The Virtue of Leadership

Ole Fogh Kirkeby

The Virtue of Leadership

Copenhagen Business School Press

The Virtue of Leadership

© Copenhagen Business School Press, 2008
Printed in Denmark by Narayana Press, Gylling
Cover design by BUSTO | Graphic Design

First edition 2008

ISBN 978-87-630-0207-3

Distribution:

Scandinavia
DBK, Mimersvej 4
DK-4600 Køge, Denmark
Tel +45 3269 7788
Fax +45 3269 7789

North America
International Specialized Book Services
920 NE 58th Ave., Suite 300
Portland, OR 97213, USA
Tel +1 800 944 6190
Fax +1 503 280 8832
Email: orders@isbs.com

Rest of the World
Marston Book Services, P.O. Box 269
Abingdon, Oxfordshire, OX14 4YN, UK
Tel +44 (0) 1235 465500, fax +44 (0) 1235 4656555
E-mail Direct Customers: direct.order@marston.co.uk
E-mail Booksellers: trade.order@marston.co.uk

All rights reserved.
No part of this publication may be reproduced or used in any form or by any means – graphic, electronic or mechanical including photocopying, recording, taping or information storage or retrieval systems – without permission in writing from Copenhagen Business School Press at www.cbspress.dk

Table of Contents

Introduction 9
Learning the Virtues of Leadership 9

PART I: LEADERSHIP 13

Chapter 1
The Leader's Relationship with Himself...................... 15

Chapter 2
What is the Good? 21
Where do we get our knowledge of the Good from? 25

Chapter 3
The Greek Square.. 31
The Good 32
The Just 36
The True 38
The Beautiful 40
Freedom 41

Chapter 4
The Leader as a Pedagogical Example 45

PART II: LEADERSHIP AND PERSONAL DEVELOPMENT.... 51

Chapter 5
The Self 53

Chapter 6
To Step into Character.. 61

PART III: ORGANIZATION AND THE OTHER 65

Chapter 7
The Social and the Event 67

Chapter 8
Experiencing the Other... 75
1. The Other as a riddle or a mystery............................. 78

2. The Other's reality is built into the forms of our communication 82
3. The event through which the Other comes into existence for me............. 87

Chapter 9
The Organizational Perspective 91

Chapter 10
The Intangible Community 101

PART IV: THE NEW THEMES OF LEADERSHIP 107

Chapter 11
Of Narratives and Leaders 109
A. The Concept of Narration 109
B. The Basis of Narration 111

Chapter 12
On Presence in Organizations 119
A. On the Inner Logic of Presence.. 119
B. Of Presence and Rhetoric 125
C. Presence and the Event.. 129

Chapter 13
Strategy and Freedom 133

PART V: THE NEW LANGUAGE OF LEADERSHIP 143

Chapter 14
The Shifting Figures of Management and Leadership 145

Chapter 15
The New Language of Leadership 157

Chapter 16
The Leader as a Spiritual Lighthouse 161

Chapter 17
The Twelve Virtues of Leadership... 169
The First Virtue of Leadership... 171
The Second Virtue of Leadership 171
The Third Virtue of Leadership 172
The Fourth Virtue of Leadership 172
The Fifth Virtue of Leadership 173
The Sixth Virtue of Leadership.. 173

Table of Contents

The Seventh Virtue of Leadership 173
The Eighth Virtue of Leadership 174
The Ninth Virtue of Leadership 175
The Tenth Virtue of Leadership 175
The Eleventh Virtue of Leadership 175
The Twelfth Virtue of Leadership 176

Introduction

Learning the Virtues of Leadership

Managers have stopped being leaders. This might be because they don't quite understand what that task implies, but their resistance to the burden of leadership may also stem from a deeper source, namely, their inability to see the point of leadership. "What good is leadership?" managers might well ask, and when we look around today's organizations, we can't really blame them. This book is nonetheless an attempt to change this attitude. It is an attempt, first, to argue for the idea of leadership as such and, next, to provide a sense of the particular qualities of a good leader. It is about both the virtue and the virtues of leadership.

Its perspective can be summarized in the image of what the baroque philosophers called the Mirror of the Prince. It is also a "protreptics" in the classical Greek sense, an injunction to the leader that he must take his life seriously, both as a leader and as a human being. It is an "encheiridion", a little handbook or manual that guides the way to being who one is.

Protreptics was a ubiquitous discipline in Greece and Rome, where philosophers and rhetoricians established what may be called "executive academies", where the top managers of that age were taught to reflect upon their own practices and to grapple with the visionary and missionary sides their upcoming activities.

"Protrepro" is Greek for the art of "turning human beings towards what is essential in their lives." Students were taught three things:
First, they were taught to reflect upon their basic attitudes in the light of the principles of the good life, and by this means to understand their responsibility for the whole of society, which was to be faced by an ethical approach to living. The Greeks, after all, took society and individual to be mutual mirrors of each other. A good and just society presupposes a good and just prince. Isocrates even described protreptrics as the art of softening the tyrant.

Second, they were taught to learn from their own experiences as leaders, to learn from history. It was all about building up a set of examples for the individual that could be transformed into a normative readiness to deal with situations as they arise in concrete events.

Third, they were taught to select their advisors (spin doctors) with care. This would allow them to control the themes that their advice would invoke, themes that were not just to be directed at the consolidation of power but also at the strengthening of the paideia, the common culture and the shared sense of the good life. Leadership must be strategic, of course, but it should also be edifying.

Within this larger project, another can be discerned. It is less institutional and more personally challenging because it brings life and leadership together in a unified whole. It is the project of becoming of worthy of the event.

This is a stoical notion, and presumably emerged from the chaos of the Hellenistic age (by the skin of its teeth), but is of enormous importance for the modern human being and for the new leader. The notion of becoming worthy of the event can be clarified using three maxims:

- It is the ability to distinguish between what is within your power and what is not.
- It is the ability to keep the secret of the event.
- It is the ability to prepare the world for the event.

This ethos is about being able to know and use one's power the right way, about knowing when the land of opportunity is a closed country. There are moral and practical ideals of reflection, mindfulness, patience, consistency, and decency in this, but also ideals of courage, persistence, cleverness and, not least, insight, circumspection and decisiveness.

Leadership is about being able to predict, anticipate, plan and survey; it is about understanding the opportunities and limits that context provides, both in our attempt to control events and in order to be able to justify one's success in making things happen. It is also about taking responsibility for one's failings.

Leadership is about not rushing to judgment, whether about people or about situations. It is about being able to read between the lines, about being able to see beneath the surface, about being able to understand the logic of history, about really being able to draw on experience, but also about being able see wholly novel and unexpected aspects of things when that is what is called for.

Finally, leadership is very much about having a project; it is about having a motivating idea. It is about holding ideals and norms that guide a campaign to be run on behalf of the community.

Introduction

These attitudes toward the event are gathered together in the ability of the individual leader to exemplify the virtues in his life and in his actions. It is about being resolute, about having a larger goal in mind, but first and foremost about being the one who first crosses the line between the tangible and the intangible, and steps into the event.

PART I

LEADERSHIP

Chapter 1

The Leader's Relationship with Himself

In what must have been Plato's last dialogue, *The Laws*, a problem is outlined that proceeds from the insight that if a state is to maintain its freedom it must see itself as being always potentially at war with other states. This applies also within a given state and in the relations between classes, between groups and within families. And it applies within each individual. The individual is forever at war with himself.

Plato continues by observing that this war can be resolved in the conquest of one's self or in a defeat to it. To conquer oneself is the greatest accomplishment of all.

This is the problem *par excellence* of leadership. The leader is at war with himself, and this is owed to the fact that before he is a leader he is a human being. Every human being is at war with himself in so far as his inner life is not mastered, in so far as no perfect harmony can be established among his impulses, his passions, his dreams and his ideas, and in so far as each of us is forever at war with everything that happens, with everything that does not live up to the project according to which we have thrown ourselves into our lives. This project is dependent on given social values, but it is no less dependent on their reflection in personal opinion.

The leader, however, is also subject to a state of war that results from his choice to enter his profession and the conditions that this choice has imposed upon him. He has taken it upon himself to administer power. He is forced into a war with himself by external factors that are at the basis of any effort to realize power, and these factors do not depend on him. They owe him nothing. More precisely, we can say that the leader is condemned to break the golden rule (which has both a positive and a negative variant: 'Do unto others as you would have them do unto you,' and 'Do not do unto others what you would not have them do unto you.') If this rule was to be followed out strictly, it would have absurd consequences in a market economy. It would imply that when one of your competitors loses a share of the market, or when one of your employees loses his job, each would value this development for its own sake, which is to say, they would see it as unconditionally justified.

If we look at the ethical and moral rules that apply to our dealings with others outside the professions, then it becomes obvious that these dealings are perceived as successful in direct proportion to the ability of the involved parties to level power off, to balance it. Our life-world is characterized by the ideal of a meeting in which the power of everyone involved is reduced to zero. The ideal love affair is understood in this way, as is the ideal friendship and even the ideal joint venture. Only those moral armatures that are founded on "natural" differences of physiology, mental capacity, experience, skill and effort, are acceptable here, but these are not understood as conduits of power because they are not immediately malleable through acts of will. We can't very well simply stop being beautiful or intelligent, can we? Not if that is what we are.

The ideal we are sketching here is the ideal of a free consensus, of consensual intimacy. It is an intimacy that is built on differences, to be sure, but on differences that do not divide. The leader, on the other hand, must presume a consensus that divides because it is he, after all, who will have the last word.

The leader is therefore by definition someone who is cut off from the means that others have to reconcile themselves with themselves, unless he appeals to a justification for the power he exercises, a justification that is not connected to his own decisions. He can, of course, claim that his decisions are necessary out of concern for the bottom line, the quality of the product, or the demands of the board. But these are all rationalizations and, finally, excuses. It does not matter how great a role these factors play in daily life nor, and perhaps especially, how they have figured in modern management thinking. They shift attention away from the heart of the matter, namely, that *the leader has chosen to lead.* This choice commits him to the confession that he has chosen a professional role that is not subject to the norms that apply to human relations in the rest of society.

We might also say that he has rejected not only the ideal that is implicit in the leveling of power, a leveling that characterizes the modern family, the modern friendship and the modern relationship, but that he has also rejected the ideal of freedom and equality that expresses the self-image of any market economy, namely, that our production and our consumption are mediated by a distribution that presumes an equality of exchange.

The Leader's Relationship with Himself

The leader is, on the contrary, forced to accomplish his inequality. He sets the agenda and he is very often able to transform criteria that had previously been perceived as "equal". After all, it is the leader who has the right to determine the value of an employee's contribution in a given context. He can in such cases denigrate that which he had previously praised.

The big issue then becomes whether there exists a way to reconcile the leader with himself. Is it part and parcel of the role of the leader that he must identify himself with power to such a degree that harmony and balance, inner peace, can only be brought about by "forgetting" one of the sides? If he forgets the values that characterize the life-world, he will become either maniacal or cynical. If he forgets the side of power he will grow tame and useless.

What is crucial here is his legitimacy.

For it is only when the rest of us suspect the contours of a balance that we become insensitive to the ways in which we are led by violence, by obscurity and by deceit. The leader must reconcile himself with power if he is to be worthy of our trust. But he can do this only if his power is justified by appeal to something other than himself. The legitimacy of the leader does not lie solely in the gesture of acknowledging his power, the act of admitting that he has power. It also lies in his ability to justify this power by appeal to something outside himself. The leader must be able to account for *why* he has chosen to seize power. And this account must always appeal to something over and above his own personal motives. Power must be chosen for the sake of something or someone.

It will simply not suffice for the leader to take his power upon himself, to stand by his will to power, unless he can find another and deeper justification for his decision to operate through power.

It is not an existentially satisfying justification for the act of seizing power that one stands by one's decision to have done so. It is a refined but finally lame excuse.

Let us look at an example of the difficulty implicit in the leader's attempt to establish and maintain an inner balance that rests on the sense of not having done wrong to anyone.

Let us imagine a company that includes among its values the notion of social responsibility. There is a desire, for example, not to dismiss employees even in cases where their jobs have been rendered obsolete by technical and economic progress. Instead, one finds them jobs elsewhere in the company, albeit on the condition that they accept the starting wage of their new function. This is construed by the employee as personally unfair and by his union representative as a political problem. But concern must also be shown for those employees who are already engaged in the transferred employee's new function. Surely their skills, which have been acquired through years of experience, entitle them to a higher wage than the newcomer? Another consideration might be rooted in the differences between old and new tasks, and therefore the time it will take to train the transferred employee in his new function.

The leader can't satisfy everyone and two forms of reasoning are confronted with each other. The first connects seniority to the total amount of time an employee has spent in the company, regardless of the tasks there undertaken. The other connects seniority to specific technical skills.

The leader can choose to support the strongest groups, which are presumably those that are not at risk of losing their jobs, or he can support those who are at such risk. Regardless of his choice, however, he will harm someone.

But he will be able to offer arguments for the decision to index wages to specific skills if he places the company in the centre of his concern. If he does the opposite, he will be suggesting that the amount of time an employee has been with the company is worth more than the contribution he is able to make (but to suggest this is also to suggest that the decision to let the employee go was justified precisely in terms of the specific contribution made).

In the great majority of cases, the leader will try to render his justification legitimate by appeal to rational arguments. The crucial basis for these arguments is provided by a concern for the well-being of the company.

Plato, too, supported this view. In *The Statesman*, he justified the importance of a strong leader in his ability to serve the interests of society as a whole.

Plato says that the leader provides *trophé*: the form of protection that a shepherd offers his sheep. The image of a shepherd is, of course, rife with ambiguity for us. There is, on the one hand, something dominating about it, something nauseatingly pastoral or simply "patriarchal" and old fashioned. On the other hand, it evokes an image of the leader that is not altogether alien to us, namely, the image of the leader as a servant of the community. We expect him, in some sense, to take care of us before he cares for himself. We, the employees, are more important to him than his own resume.

Plato divides *trophé* into two further functions of leadership: *epimeleia*, or "cura" in Latin, meaning "care", and *therapeuo*, "seduction" in Latin, meaning "the will to heal". In organizational contexts, then, we are talking about the motivation to take care of oneself. The Latin translation, evoking shades of "seduction", shows us that this concept is ambiguous. Is it necessary to be "seduced" into an understanding of one's own interests and needs? Perhaps it is: if, for example, the structures and management practices within the organization have not previously made this possible. We know how difficult it can be to adjust to a whole new range of personal freedom.

The leader becomes the obvious representative both of a more genuine sense of community and of what the organization, given the right conditions, could turn out to be. He seizes upon the "life" or "spirit" of the organization, the ghost, as it were, in the machine, one that all too often ossifies when it tries to manifest itself through explicit and implicit rules, in tacit duress, in precedent, in "the way we usually do it" and "this is how it is done around here".

In this regard, Plato emphasizes that, while law is essential to any community, the leader stands above the law (he is often himself a lawmaker) because he can resolve ambiguities created by the law itself and because he has a sense of how the law can be applied in novel situations. The leader is ideally the prime exponent of that force which serves as the animating principle of the whole organization.

We can easily transfer Plato's reasoning from the community of the state to that of the firm – though we must naturally make a few historical qualifications in relation to the state as a framework for group survival and in relation to all those minorities that Athenian society has simply marginalized.

The leader, then, holds power, and therefore enjoys a position of justified authority; first, because he possesses insight into the structure of the organization, its principles, its values; second, because he can construe these in the light of the survival of the whole; and, third because he has the ability to transform the goals of the community.

The leader is not just the one who can settle conflicts that arise where criteria begin to spin their wheels. He can also introduce new criteria and new laws.

But what is the Great Criterion that legitimates his status in general? The answer is to be found in his insight.

The only thing that can ease the burden of the cross of power that he bears, the force of the war within the leader himself, is that insight which justifies itself through an intimate familiarity with the history and purpose of the company.

But we will of course have to understand *what* the company is, that is, *who* it is for, before we can understand its purpose.

And we can only answer this question when we have become capable of determining the content of the criterion that the company and its leaders can and should be judged by. What is the Good?

Chapter 2

What is the Good?

To enter into arguments for and against the quality of human nature is to embark upon an almost wholly useless adventure. Studies of primitive societies since the 1700s have shown that while primitive peoples do sometimes demonstrate greater group solidarity than "moderns" they are more often unspeakably gruesome in their treatment of other small societies, tribes, clans, groups, and so forth, even where they have known of each other's existence for centuries and are perhaps related.

History shows us with all the clarity we might desire that "Man to Man is an arrant Wolfe," as the English baroque philosopher Thomas Hobbes put it. "To speak impartially," he said, "both sayings are very true; That *Man to Man is a kind of God*; and that *Man to Man is an arrant Wolfe*. The first is true, if we compare Citizens amongst themselves; and the second, if we compare Cities." That is, man is not as a wolf to other men *within his established community*; as citizen among other citizens, man is to man "a kind of god". It is only outside the community that man's lupine qualities are most conspicuous. Indeed, if the Greeks had one message to leave to posterity, beyond the ideal of the city state and the idea of philosophy, then it would be the insight that human goodness presupposes upbringing and education: in short, "enlightenment" – or what we today might call "life long learning". Goodness requires community.

This insight was then taken over by Christianity, amplifying its implications in the concept of original sin and in teachings about the sad fate of unbaptized children. The symbolic initiation into the Christian community of believers in baptism, the reception of "the word" ("kerygma") in the form of the sermon, the spiritual apprenticeship under Martin Luther's small catechism: all these were prerequisites for abandoning one's nature. Faith in an amiable and noble will is an invention of the eighteenth century, an invention of men who had never encountered representatives of other cultures save for pipe-smoking Indian chiefs, Chinese sages and pitiable slaves and servants. The construal of primitive man as a counter-image to the evils of capitalist civilization, however, was just as understandable as the construal of childhood as innocence.

As history has sadly shown, the ulterior motive that underlies the construction of these "natures", each of which represents a lack of individualism, a lack of egoism or sense of "enlightened self-interest" and a lack of "refined" cultural needs, is to prepare the ground for the puppets and cannon fodder of totalitarian societies. The ideal of personal "authority", as articulated by Kant during the enlightenment, is the only antidote against this poison. The naïve victim of indoctrination can be liberated only through criticism and the intelligent love of one's neighbor.

We live in a culture that must still be considered Christian because its humanist ideals are intertwined with its fundamental values; and whether or not we are Christian in any ritualized sense of the word, we know the good through our basic Christian values. Since these values are identical with the norms of Western culture, we are consigned to find our bearings within a set of essentially Christian values when answering the question of where the Good comes from.

Our fundamental Christian values emphasize a universal humanity beyond the doctrines and dogmas of one or another orthodoxy. Such orthodoxies give us the impression that the individual is a creature that has nothing to do with cultural and historical values beyond those that make up the canons of the Holy Scriptures and are sanctioned by the institutionalized practice of faith, hope and love in the major religions.

It has therefore been possible to "secularize" Christianity in the sense that a humanistic image of man has been drawn from it, one that stresses the virtues found in the New Testament—first and foremost the love of man—and an openness with regard to the interpretation of major Greek "ideas", namely, the Good, the True and the Just. Christianity, after all, emerges from its Jewish and Hellenistic inheritance. The apostle Paul, who wrote his epistles in the demotic Greek of the streets long *before* the gospels had been written, liberated the Jewish intellectual dowry from its fixation on "the law", in the name of a stoic global order, that excludes no one, leaves no one "outside", except those that either haven't heard or don't want to listen to "the word", "logos".

Dogmatic Christianity is not an especially inspiring notion in a multicultural and multi-ethnic society. But the Christian message remains strong even today, because it underscores responsibility with respect to the individual, the community (a community that in principle includes *everyone* who wants to join it), and oneself.

Like I say, the Christian message rests on Judaism, Greek philosophy and Greek mysticism (Gnosticism). Throughout the evolution of Christianity, which is granted its status as the official religion of Roman society only in the fourth century, we see a continuous emphasis on loyalty to the community. This was in many ways natural. Christians were fugitives and minorities whose internal cohesion was simply necessary to their survival. That is how the early history of the Church began: with a sense of responsibility to what Cicero dubbed the "communitas", a sense of community that implies an absolute commitment. He was thinking of Roman society, of course, and had never heard of Christ, but it was nonetheless precisely this community that could house the Christian "spirit", or "ethos", and it was here that it could grow.

Christianity repeats the insight that the major Greek philosophers and the Roman "disciples", such as Cicero, Seneca and Marcus Aurelius, founded their lives upon: the individual can only improve himself.

When Søren Kierkegaard, several thousand years later, underscores our subjectivity, it is precisely in an attempt to revamp this attitude of unconditional commitment to the spirit of an original society, and precisely the non-Christian society. It is a community that has been perverted into a religion of habit and transformed into a state religion, but which in its original conception was about unconditional faith, about loving your neighbor as yourself, and about a living, spontaneous fellowship.

The "asceticism", the set of spiritual exercises, the arduous work upon one's own self, that both the Greeks and the Christians sought to shape their lives by, has much to teach us even today. It is about conquering a set of paradoxes about *how* a human being personally and seriously appropriates the Good, and to such a degree that he becomes one with it.

Aristotle would put the paradox as follows. In order to be able to do the right thing, we will have to know what is good. But in order to know what is good, we must have done some good, i.e., we must already have done the right thing.

The apostle Paul would say that in order know faith we must practice it in each and every detail of our lives. But in order to put our faith into practice we must have it.

The solution to both problems is now and has always been the same: formative education, or the inculcation of values.

But it is essential that the contents of this edification, this moral apprenticeship, are fundamentally different for Aristotle and Paul. The latter proceeds from a revelation, which is to say, he works with hard and fast boundaries between good and not good. Aristotle eschews with resolute finality any determination of the content of the good, but he nonetheless retains the idea of the Good as a "regulative principle", just as his teacher Plato had before him. It is a set of ideals that one can improve one's sensitivity to through the course of a life. The same conclusion emerged when philosophy began to free itself from Christianity, albeit while remaining anchored to its premises. Immanuel Kant, too, was forced to declare that the idea of the Good is not available to experience and can therefore never be monopolized by any single faction.

Edification consists of upbringing and education; the first major work of philosophical pedagogy is Augustine's *The Teacher* (*De Magistro*). Christianity provides us with the first comprehensive well-organized, goal-oriented program of life long learning. Edification, inculcation and education merge into one and are set in relation to the crux of the matter, namely, whether one is involved in an apprenticeship to another or exclusively to oneself. It is important, also, whether the master is a friend, a teacher, a priest or an estranged authority. Or whether "he" is a collection of words—a book that can be consulted according to one's personal convictions and interpreted according to the dictates of the heart.

But edification demands guidance in any case – even today when self-study programs and distance learning have become commonplace.

This is why the apostle Paul writes letters to his congregations in faraway places. It is also the reason that the Greeks established, first, their philosophical academies and, later, in the Hellenistic era, campuses where a personally informed apprenticeship could take place. We know that the rabbinic orders established such places in the Baltics and in Poland: a well developed system that the Nazis undertook to destroy with great finality (if the Cossacks and commissars hadn't already managed to do so). Pythagoras made so little of his authority that he only taught at night, where no one could see him, or with his back to his audience when he lectured. This is the sort of teacher and teaching that the ancient Greeks sought and, to this day, Zen Buddhism takes a similar approach. During the Middle Ages, Christians who had the education and the means to do so, traveled to the major cities—Paris in most cases—where they could find themselves a teacher or master (the "magistro" of Augustine's book about the teacher). From the 1700s and onwards, Hassidic Judaism also encouraged young believers to seek out more or less famous teachers (rabbis) in order to live with them, and to learn the scriptures from them. This personal relationship between teacher and student is no longer common in Western, European societies. This is a shame, because it provides a setting in which to communicate personal experiences along with philosophical and disciplinary problems through the authority that a long and deeply engaged practice makes possible. It is the inexorable core of all learning, and we might have to understand the mentor relationships that arise between young and old leaders as an attempt to revive this tradition.

Christianity and Judaism had this in common: they both cultivated the insight that developing the Good in oneself is a matter of finding a balance between one's personal efforts and one's dependence on the community. The centre of this balance is the act of engaging oneself fully in a norm and thereby to realize it in thought and action. And they know that this evolutionary process is tied to the creative reconciliation of thought and desire. It is about learning how to feel what one thinks, how to do what one wants—precisely, the Good—because the thought, the commitment and the norm have found their way into each fiber, each fold and each layer of the body.

The big question now is: How is modern man to learn of the Good? And in our context: What kind of apprenticeship can the leader enroll in?

What constitutes the leader's community?

Where do we get our knowledge of the Good from?
A.   We know the Good from the Golden Rule, that is, from the experience we draw out of our social contexts, where we identify ourselves with others. Em-pathy (from the Greek for "into" and "feeling") is an unavoidable aspect of everyday experience. But the fact that we can make ourselves immune to it shows that it is not just an expression of our nature but also presupposes a social impulse, provided by upbringing. The demands of our empathy are often easy to explain away. We can let norms that either make too little of the Golden Rule or too much of the "business at hand" take control of our inner dialogue, our soul's conversation with itself. We can, for example, tell ourselves that the dysfunctional employee is in every case either stupid or lazy. We can disengage our empathy when someone demands that we try to understand his situation. Or we can say that he belongs to another religion or another ideology, another race or another culture, one that frees

us from the obligation to approach him on an equal footing with ourselves.

It is no coincidence that two major works addressing the theory of our possibilities for mutual understanding—Adam Smith's *The Theory of Moral Sentiments* and David Hume's *An Enquiry Concerning the Principles of Morals* arrive in the same decade, the 1750s. After all, the creation of a capitalistic society and its democratic institutions has the effect of eroding the standing valorization of the Golden Rule, which characterizes feudal societies. It is for this reason that a moral or ethical code of conduct must be worked out, one that underscores the importance of an authentic, empathetic relationship to other people and a responsible relation to the community in spite of the indifference of the markets and the war of all against all. The idea that everyone can relate to everyone else, precisely because everyone is relevant, begins to take hold in spite of the poor and huddled masses that become fodder for work houses, factories and armies, and in spite of an often selfish, self-righteous and arrogant elite.

B. We know the Good from the example set us by people that have influenced us immediately through relatively close contact: politicians, brothers in arms, freedom fighters, selfless and ordinary people who are actively involved in our everyday lives, where unexpected generosity is so often displayed.

C. We know the Good from philosophy and from our educational institutions. That is, we know it from a series fundamental maxims, principles, arguments and declarations (of human rights, of human duties), that is, from reasonably clear attitudes that mark the boundary between a humane approach to social living in its many oppositions.

D. We know it from theories of the state, from works of history, from biographies, from all the theoretical and "empirical" summaries of the structures, deeds and personalities that repress or liberate our common humanity. Allegories about the capacity of power to corrupt had already been written in the middle ages. Dante's *Divine Comedy* is the most famous of these, written at the beginning of the fourteenth century. The Christian narratives were developed during the baroque through allegories of power and its impotence, the vanity of human wishes, and turned into positive models of society in which feudal hierarchies were softened and "the theatre of life" was partly stripped of its gruesome arbitrariness with respect to the individual—as we find it in Thomas More's *Utopia* from 1516. The novels of the baroque focus on a negative display of the immorality of power, and examples from the Roman Empire are employed as deterrents in the history books. But the most important development is probably the rise of the idea of natural law: the stoic idea that every human being has been given by birth a right to fair treatment and equality of opportunity. In the idea of natural rights we find the beginnings of the theory of a state founded on the rights of man and, with this, the beginnings of the idea of a democratic society. That is, we find here an attempt to describe in a careful and "scientific" manner the potential of the idea of the Good as a principle of social organization. Realistic attempts to guide the taming of mankind's selfish nature, through state constitutions, as in Thomas Hobbes' famous *Leviathan* from 1651, and their relation to the temper of the Enlightenment, will lead to the creation of the conceptual basis of the modern constitution, as in Montesquieu's *Spirit of the Law*, from 1748. But there were also more personal declarations of commitment to the idea of the Good. Pascal's *Thoughts*, from the middle of the 1600s, Spinoza's *Ethics*, published posthumously at the close of the seventeenth century, and Leibniz's *Theodicy*, from 1710, made decisive philosophical contributions to the preservation of the idea of the good.

E. We know the good from religion, especially the doctrine of tolerance that we find in secular Christianity, with its emphasis on the love of one's neighbor and the right to a personal faith. G. E. Lessing, the German writer and critic, developed such a doctrine in the middle of the eighteenth century and by this means inaugurated the Enlightenment.

F. But the most genuine and the greatest lessons in goodness are to be found in the examples and stories that have been handed down under the auspices of the Christian religions. We know of the good from the gospels and from the accounts of people who lived in accordance with their faith—most of the days of the year bear the name of such "holy" men. We know of the ideal of the gospels from countless novels, short stories and stage dramas that compose their variations on this theme. I need only remind the reader of Victor Hugo's novel *Les Miserables*, which has been made into movies, mini series and, of course, a musical.

The Virtue of Leadership

G. And we know of the good from that more or less believable stream of documentation and discussion we meet in the mass media. Here deeds, people and institutions are continuously deemed to be "in" or "out", whether the justification of the war in Iraq (which in the final analysis is about what is good for the people of that country) or the surveillance of sex offenders.

H. And last but not least, we know of the Good by way of serious art. Not just from literature, but from film, dance, music, and the plastic arts. Aesthetics draw their force from an ethos that expresses an ideal "humanity", one that is never blind to the relativity of this notion, how dependent on context it is, and how difficult it is to realize it on the basis of the animal in each of us and the accidents that still, despite the advances in information technologies, characterize the day-to-day affairs of the individual. And it is from the arts that we can learn about the fatal consequences of narrow-mindedness, especially that particular form of spiritual myopia fostered by social groups, and the ways in which the Good is placed in the service of power through micro-technological tricks that span the continuum from self-deception at home to self-righteousness abroad.

Through all these teachings and lessons a common sense, or human understanding, is fostered that is possessed of a strong and differentiated, critical and sensitive potential to distinguish between good and evil.

Since the leader is a citizen and part of a cultural and historical community, he is, as a human being, naturally subject to the weight of the same sources of information.

But where is he to learn of the connection between leadership and the Good? Where is he to learn about leadership in the spirit of the Good?

As I see it, the only one he can learn from in this regard, or learn from with any degree of seriousness, is himself, even if the example of other leaders can help him on his way.

He must, in this sense, be "primitive"; that is, he must cultivate the arts of self-examination and self-criticism, or what the stoics called "zetesis" and "krisis", which they had honed to perfection. He must, like the stoics, begin each new day with his own self, and must leave no stone unturned in a fundamentally self-critical attitude that eschews all compromise and even the best of excuses.

What is the Good?

The leader, then, must *create himself* each morning, each moment, but *self-creation* is just as tricky a phenomenon as it is complicated, not just because it is scarred like any other buzzword by overuse but because it is so very difficult to discover what exactly it means.

First of all, it is only possible to create oneself on a cultural and historical background that is based on abilities, talents and competences, is based on one's particular psychological constellation, is based on one's experience, is based on one's memories, is based on one's knowledge, and is based on the goals one is able to set for oneself through the ideals one has been given and given oneself access to. In this sense, the idea of the Good and its concrete expression in "the good life" often becomes diffuse, subjective or dogmatic.

Add to this that you can never create yourself in isolation. Self-creation is not the pure development of natural talents but a process that only makes sense in a particular social context. One always creates oneself *for* someone and *with* someone, always in regard *to* something.

Close relationships—in the family, at work, etc.—is the precondition of self-creation. But relationships can be many things.

Certainly, they exist as a system in the sense of "formal structures" where power is distributed through authority, history, influence, information, network and complex feedback mechanisms between respect and recognition.

But "under" these systems we again find "wholes" that consist of communities created by the opportunities we have to realize ourselves, spanning from common interests to intellectual themes, collector's items, "perversions" and cultural hobbies to communities shaped by a belief in a purpose in life and work and communities that arise more or less spontaneously on the basis of "history", shared "chemistry" or a shared "fate".

All these living or organic communities, which are often informal in nature, set their mark on all organizations. They live, so to speak, "under the surface", and they are what the leader must establish contact with, what he must both challenge and reconcile himself with, when he arrives in a new company or problems arise in his own.

Since the beginning of Western culture in Greece, 2500 years ago, a core of concepts have determine the content of the Good by always appearing alongside it. These concepts express a balance between that which the individual alone can seek within a *normative* perspective and that which society or the community can emphasize as its own ideal foundation. The *normative* refers to *norms* or ideals are living but open "values" that mark the boundary with the absolute or unconditional. They are connected to very abstract concepts, which are the anchor points of Western culture that it must interpret on a daily basis as individuals make use of them in their lives. These concepts thus guide any process of self-development and self-creation, if it is not to be egoistic and empty.

Inspired by Plato's dialogue, *The Sophist*, I have chosen to call the mutual constellation of these concepts, the Great Square, or the Greek Square.

It is important to point out immediately that no one can claim copyright to the precise or "dogmatic" content of the normative concepts. What the German philosopher Immanuel Kant said in his *Critique of Judgment* also counts here:

> *an idea of reason (. . .) is a concept that cannot be countered by any intuition (an idea of the imagination). (§49)*

The Good lives behind a curtain that has not yet been torn from the altar.

Chapter 3

The Greek Square

But how can the leader find his bearings beyond the pitfalls of strategy? These pitfalls include the temptation to engage in cynically motivated moral embellishment, as well as post-fact rationalizations, which justify the will to power by appeal to the common good. What is the intellectual basis that will ensure that his speech is unambiguous and honest, since his thoughts are such? It is his ability to relate to the Great Square.

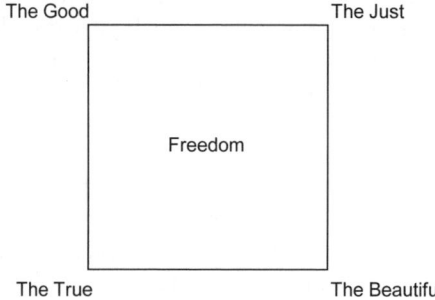

This is also the Greek philosophers' great square and is thus the normative foundation of Western culture.

In the center of this square is "freedom", for it is only possible to approach the norms seriously if one chooses them on the basis of free choice and thus whole heartedly.

As already noted, what is crucial to these four points and their center is that they do not function in visual form, since a fixed visual image or picture would make them too concrete and thus bind them to a fixed construction or interpretation.

These four points are concepts. They are units of meaning – doors that open into worlds of meaning and which should be explored over and over again by anyone who uses them. To explore them demands courage, the will to pay the price, but this exploration also demands humility and unselfishness. In a sense, one must hear their "calling" in order to come into genuine contact with these norms. They can never be interpreted authoritatively, and from this stems their normativity since the normative expresses a boundary of thought which must be sought yet never crossed. The normative includes ideals, so-called regulative ideas, which constitute and serve as the compass for any serious character to follow.

They are thus simultaneously individual and collective in size.

Let us look at the points of the square, one by one, and illustrate the contours of their content.

The Good

The concept 'the good' is a pillar in Western thought about the world and in our ethics. The good is called *agathon* in Greek and "bonus" or "bonum" in Latin. The span of this concept is quite large. It does not merely denote an essential quality of God. The conception of God's absolute goodness, according to which he is in fact "plusquam bonus", i.e., "more than good", permeates the theology and philosophy of the middle Ages. But the good also denotes a human virtue; it constitutes a subjective goal for each individual through (his) tangible actions. The good is at the same time characterized by numerous attempts to define it precisely within the various philosophical, theological, and social–utopian systems; it is also characterized by a great vagueness within the world of philosophy and in ordinary usage.

In modernity the good is increasingly characterized by the following contradiction. On the one hand, there is a push to establish universal norms for the good in line with a growing awareness of the possibility of a real world community or global society. Here the good is bound to the lowest common denominator and is expressed by the so-called golden rule found in its negative and most viable version ("do not do unto others what you do not wish them to do unto you") and to the charters of international human rights. On the other hand, the task of fulfilling the good on an everyday basis is left increasingly to the individual carry out in a personal manner. Seen in this light the concept of the good becomes doubly functionalistic. It is used to regulate global communication, and it is used as a substitute for an authoritatively propagated religious experience.

But just as the good may serve as a compass for the individual's actions, it is also a criterion by which all people from all walks of life are increasingly being judged. This also applies to the leader.

If the organization is perceived as a micro-state, it cannot form its own laws and rules for the Good. Rather, it is compelled not only to actualize a universal understanding of the good but should actually be on the cutting edge of this process. This means that responsibility becomes a part of the leader's agenda. Responsibility is the way by which we "answer" the demands that are made of our humanity, which are expressed by our conscience, yet is fostered by a global respect for nature, people and culture. We are today witnessing a mushrooming of this respect.

Responsibility becomes a very complicated concept because it demands not only a heightened sensibility toward all "worlds" other than one's own, but because sensibility depends on an intelligent and inspired effort. It is really of little use for a leader to adhere to the formal codes of practice in order to administer the interests of "sustainability". It is, rather, about being ahead of the game regarding the evolution of a new and more careful relationship to that nature to which the sustainability of production refers.

When the most recent studies of young leaders' focus areas show that empathy is highly prioritized, it is a clear indication that leaders under the age of forty navigate in search of the good. Empathy is the anticipatory, warm, and understanding approach that is taken toward another person (here, the employee). Although incorporating empathy among may be another matter altogether since this demands experience, tact and a realistic outlook, these studies leave us with a clear signal that the business world is no longer a closed world, hidden behind the walls of the factory where power makes its own rules. The private ownership of places, machines and know-how no longer legitimates an exemption from the norms that govern ethical relations between people. These norms continue set the agenda for our relationships with one another.

The new leader must thus understand himself in light of the possibility of a new kind of life behind the factory walls, a life where the social solidarity of work is much more intimate and therefore much more personally binding and directed toward the personal. There are a number of reasons for this. A more personal, more human march of civilization has become both the right and duty of all educated people in the new millennium, because otherwise they (the educated) cannot enjoy the fruits of the culturally differentiated "good life" that progress makes possible and because they cannot by any other means attain a sufficient degree of variation to encompass the broad spectrum of competences that is demanded of them. There is also the fact that the walls of the factory have been dismantled by phenomena like the formation of networks, knowledge sharing, the tying of know-how and competence to employees who themselves plan their career paths, which is to say, who are embarked on an adventure that will take them through many companies other than your own in a lifetime. And there is the aggressive and promising public sphere currently being created by the Internet. Any company can at any time be exposed by grassroots movements, by the press and exhibited by its admirers and its passionate supporters.

For this reason, it is imperative that both private and public organizations establish proactive strategies with the aim of "benchmarking" themselves as trustworthy partners and dependable suppliers, as effective producers and service providers, and as exciting workplaces. All this suggests the use of rhetoric to communicate in a way that ignites passion, awakens enthusiasm, but also attaches convincing arguments and delivers results that build confidence. The new use of rhetoric is called "branding" and its novelty does not change the fact that it is still possible to differentiate between a rhetoric that stands in the service of the good and one does not.

The *brand* is a double-edged sword. Not only is the concept itself in its basic meaning aggressive and condescending toward its potential target audience—for it evokes the image of fire branding the hind quarters of a cow—it has a high ante. What is won or lost in the way of public image during a given marketing campaign also sets the agenda for inner organizational success in retaining, motivating and recruiting desirable employees. When everyone "brands", the organization becomes extremely sensitive for the overall impression it manages to leave on the basis of its whole sum of good intentions. The intentions behind it might in any case also foster at once idealized and totalitarian images of the company.

If the organization is evaluated on the basis of its social responsibilities—that is, on the seriousness of its products and services, its ability to attract and retain women in management positions, its political justice, its investment and acquisition strategies, its treatment of the disabled, and its ability to integrate ethnic minorities—then it must steer toward to the good.

The problem is that the when companies compete to make a good impression in public as an organizational space the internal reality of which is marked by strong moral integrity and clear ethical considerations, then both deceptiveness and half-heartedness come to weigh heavily upon the situation. To cheat on the scales here is only to cheat oneself.

The new leader must therefore be *cultivated* in the sense that he must be able to apply his knowledge (the result of his education, i.e., his culture) in a context consisting of diverse *attitudes*. Management of course still involves a basic craft element. One must have a working understanding of accounting, have knowledge of micro-economics in theory and practice and still be able to make and read something that looks like a *balanced scorecard*. But the slide from craft to attitude is currently in the process of transforming the content of the strategic context of leadership.

It ought to be obvious by now that there is something strongly functionalistic about our approximation of the Good. Companies are not altruistic educational institutions, but businesses, and public institutions also navigate in these waters. The power that consumers, employees, and investors have today, in accord with never before seen degree of publicity around all of the organization's actions, whether as seen from the outside or the inside, put the leader in a very difficult dilemma. He must make decisions that pit the long-term up against the short-term again and again. Economic decisions, which are evident in the short-term, can turn out to be fatal because they don't foster an image of the organization as a cooperative and well-meaning partner for the consumer. There doesn't seem to be choice any longer in questions of whether to refuse to recall two-hundred cars due to a very small and nonrecurring defect which may lead to unwanted publicity where notions of irresponsibility, cynicism, and lack of service-mindedness may result or just to accept the economic loss. Nor does it seem obvious that one can motivate employees to make an extra effort by saying, "We've got to save 10% of last year's budget," or "In two years we've got to bring the bottom line up by 3%." It seems that we need another kind of language where one can talk about being "…the best of the best *for* nation, for the environment, or for the society of the future."

Similarly, there are new demands being made today for sponsorship. This is about much more than just logos on sweatshirts. When The Danish Telephone Corporation introduces the concept of "children's day" and creates an internal sponsorship strategy where every employee receives a day off with full pay to do something beneficial for children, it's a signal from an intelligently led organization that knows which way the wind is blowing. Anyone, no matter how obsessed we are with professional sports, can see that the needs of children's are more important than opium for the masses – these sporting events being a concoction of deadly seriousness and jocular spectacle.

Responsibility brings obligations with it and, by the same token, landmark or "defining" actions of responsibility on the part of the leader obligates the partners of the organization. Therefore, the leader's ability to treat his employees based on the criteria of the Good is a crucial parameter of competitive advantage. The leader must exhibit a sensitivity for the fact that employees are people too. There's no way around it. The Good is never actualized, however, unless it is connected to the corner of the great square called *justice*. As employees, we want recognition the recognition *we deserve*. We don't want to be recipients of a charity that stems from the troubled consciences of the powers that be.

The Just
Justice, then, is the second corner. Justice can't be understood in a work-related context unless it is developed in relation to the practice of *recognition*.

In an organizational context, we can start by saying that recognition, in relation to partners, is the exact opposite of seduction.

Recognition, after all, recognizes both the person and the ardor of personality.

Recognition is an attitude toward the other, one that refuses to regard the other as a means. The other is always an end. So the seducer, in all of his manifestations, is shunted onto a sidetrack. Naturally, this does not mean that recognition doesn't have its *own* school. Within the history of philosophy recognition is a concept associated with the name of the German philosopher, G.W.F. Hegel – as we'll see in the following chapters. He deduces recognition from a history whose fundamental actors are masters and slaves. The lesson here lies in learning that their respective positions are mutually dependent. The master needs a slave in order to feel like a master; he needs a subservient mirror. Conversely, the slave requires a master in order to understand himself as the subordinate. But in due time this experience of dependence on positions of power by functional approaches led to the possibility of a confrontation with these roles. Recognition contains the seed of freedom—a seed that consists of their shared sense of humanity. The master will only become human when he sees himself in the slave, and the slave can only become human when he sees himself in the master. The human tragedy is transformed into a human comedy: we can switch roles because we wear social masks.

Removing the masks, however, requires more than just a personal psychological flair for changing roles. It requires a change of structure, the removal of power and the development of rights and duties. It requires *training in the humanities*, pure and simple.

Recognition, like a seismographic instrument that registers even the tiniest quakes in the relations between people, conveys the possibility to develop a sense of the subtle balance between the individual's ability to administer the tension between *rights and duties*—whether he is a leader or an employee. One of the most important tasks for the leader today is to create a free space within the organization that allows it to develop this tension and direct it toward harmony. It is the leader's task to establish the balance between what the organization can do for employees by giving them work, fostering social bonds, opportunities to develop their talents—to learn, to shine—and the employees' abilities and will to strengthen the organization through passion, innovative will-power, attention and precision.

The clearest picture of how the good and the just appears in the leader's identity may be characterized by his ability to be present in the situation.

In any case, the way by which recognition manifests itself is deeply connected with the recognizer's ability to be present. In his presence, I am seen and heard by the leader. This flair for administrating the means that comprise the somewhat intangible ability to praise another, an ability that certain leaders possess, and which is best understood as a talent for understatement, installs an enormous potential between people.

Justice must permeate organizations.

Justice is bound to systems of recognition that can be particularly clever and which can work, even though they're relatively formalized – like Ericsson's monetary reward for an employee if he recruits a new one, or like their award given to the year's internal innovator. But the entire system of monetary rewards and fringe benefits is nothing compared to the "social recognition" which consists of an employee being distinguished within the organization for his approach or his efforts.

But justice is connected to yet another phenomenon: the possibility of criticism.

Criticism is probably the most delicate organizational phenomenon. It is what is most difficult for the leader to handle properly.

Boxes set up in a company's cafeteria which serve the purpose of allowing employees to submit slips of paper that criticize their organization and the leadership of that organization naturally constitutes a start, but only if they're not anonymous. For it is in the possibility of criticizing without repercussions, indeed, of being met by virtue of one's will to criticize, that characterizes a decent organization. Criticism is probably one of the most creative phenomena we know, but it is only creative if it can occur in the light of tolerance. We build the community by removing all the superfluous material, so that eventually the sculpture that was hidden within the company may be revealed in all of its beauty.

"Criticism" is normative in its nature. Genuine criticism goes back to the idea of the good. It doesn't content itself with superficial cost effective criteria and random fashionable perspectives. There are large and small critical activities and small and large critical campaigns inside all surviving organizations. But the larger, more obvious critical campaigns are generally carried out with an iron fist by new company directors, leaders, or by "surgical" consultants who are called in to assist them. In such instances, a "regimen" is always proposed, by which the organization can regain its strength. However, one should realize that the ensuing asceticism, which takes the form of restrictions and cutbacks doesn't live up to the original meaning of the Greek concept of *askesis*. After all, *askesis* denotes that set of mental or spiritual exercises that a person has at his disposal in order to train his thoughts and his will to obtain the good. *Askesis* involves hard work, not the declaration of abstinence on behalf of others.

This careful "little" *askesis* is associated with a criticism whose objective is to strengthen the organization's intellectual and volitional potential. This is not always achieved by heavy-handedly swinging a global blade. The organization's body is sensitive, but this sensitivity often constitutes its actual strength. Fixation on the bottom line, initiatives based on rough figures and simple panic attacks have destroyed the potential of many businesses. The gold standard of the competences of the company is not to be found in the individual employees but in that technical and emotional bonding that is laboriously established between them.

In this sense, justice within organizations depends on the creation of and adherence to a *free space*. The air that one breathes in this room is called *trust*.

The True
The true, the third corner of the great square, refers to the organization's ability to create a product or service which corresponds to the best grounded and most up to date scientific knowledge. Research within companies and through the so-called triple helix—the interaction of research institutions, public authorities and the business com-

munity—becomes a growing part of all organizations' innovative conduct. But research involves many elements, it has become essential to develop knowledge policy in step with the accumulation of research results, as Mogens Weinreich, the administrative director of the SAS Institute, has emphasized this in connection with the implementation of databases and computer-based management tools.

A knowledge policy is not just about the know-how that is demanded by production and service procedures, procedures that the organization should of course possess. It is about the whole of organizational experience.

The new leader should actually be a scientist in the classical sense—a renaissance man who can assess the relevance of all types of knowledge within his organizational universe. Naturally, he needs to make use of experts who can advise him about technological knowledge; it is impossible today to survey the developments within a specific knowledge area in its entirety. The leader who attempts this will be consumed from the inside by the complexities of role of "engineer".

But the fundamental dimension of knowledge is and remains normative, i.e., it should be formed by the light that is refracted by the first two corners of the great square: the good and the just. The business community's criteria of relevance in relationship to the development of knowledge are naturally pragmatic, even though the manufacturing that is done by, e.g., Novo Nordisk and COWI has clear humanistic objectives. But a pragmatic concern in and of itself, i.e., the perspective according to which the extent and quality of the application of knowledge is decisive, is not a free-floating one. It is about utility, to be sure, but utility is in turn always about norms. What is useful is "of use" to someone and for something—primarily to some end. It is from the world of the good and the just that our objectives, and therefore our objects of knowledge, really derive their legitimacy.

In markets where competition is increasingly about the quality of a product, technical perfection, understood in a minimalist sense, is obviously a phantasm. Perhaps the worth of technical perfection applies to certain parts of the production process but the properties of the final product and the final service is ultimately decided by the relation these products have to people's "lifestyles"—to culturally formed preferences and to fundamental ideas about the role of "prosthetics" in our lives. Prostheses relate to ways in which products are natural extensions of our bodies. Otherwise, our Jeeps would still be made without suspension systems and our thermos would look as the have since the 1920s.

In this century, where both businesses and the public sector are increasingly obligated by the circulation of information, the truth is bound to the linguistic discursive, metaphorical and narrative expressions through which it is conveyed.

The importance of the story as a means of conveying the truth about the organization illustrates precisely how inseparable the true is from the normative, from the good and from a perspective that summarizes events through a historicity that derives its impact from the auspices of justice. You can't run sweatshops in New Mexico if you want to sell sneakers to people who are committed to social equality on a global scale, and then simply conceal it in the glorification of the organization's "greatness", the tale of its victory, as Nike has been accused of doing.

In this sense, truth in the business community filters into the fourth corner of the great square—the beautiful. In so far as the truth about the product is founded in its measurable technical qualities and its scientific specifications, whether in relation to its intrinsic quality or its effect on people and the environment, then this truth is always in need of mediation by the aesthetics of the product.

The Beautiful

Beauty has as little to do with seduction as recognition. If beauty is the packaging of truth, then it is only because it emphasizes those aspects of the product or service that stand up to the test of its normative fiber—because it draws attention to its association with the good, in other words.

The beautiful is found where we meet it earnestly: in genuine art—revolutionary (in a critical-utopian sense), transformative, strong in its presence, uncompromising and deeply, deeply normative. Art dreams of justice and fulfillment; it is found in its alliance with the hideous, where it hides beneath the surface of nonsense.

In the final analysis, it is actually possible to think of the Beautiful as a particularly advanced and critical way of affirm the Good.

Cicero says:

> *This harmony of inner being, in which there is no contradiction between logos and the instincts, constitutes the 'beauty' of the soul. This is nothing other than what the Greeks have always called 'the beautiful' in the highest sense of the word, the ethical good that unfolds itself in particular within the community. It is*

by this life in the community that rational beings are disposed in advance. [Cicero, De finibus, III, 17, 21.] [1]

First and foremost, the leader should of course be able to separate one thing from another and good art from superficial sophistication. And it is difficult to make the distinction today, where art runs rampant, and where it employs means that overstep the boundaries of its earlier sanctuaries.

When you wrap a parliament in plastic, when you exhibit excrement, when you glorify the commonplace by painting cans of soup, then art, paradoxically, ceases to be a stage set and turns toward exactly what the leader's working life is all about: *to find a new form for one's actions.*

Any innovator and any designer in any advertisement agency and anyone who is oriented toward the optimization of his "performance" knows first hand that art struggles with form, with expression. They are oriented each in their own way by following a criterion that can easily be called "the beautiful".

But the leader can only be a convincing performer who employs a whole range of effects if he is able to demonstrate that the end only justifies means that are themselves able to justify ends that can bear their justification.

Although it can be difficult, most people have a built-in sense of criticism that allows us to see through all of the situations where the form of human action compensates for its lack of content.

The ability to situate the beautiful in the great square fosters a sober sense of the aesthetic that allows us to resist the temptation of seduction, of the cheap tricks and superficial effects that may be a hit in the short term, but in the long terms of consequences of which we'll pay dearly for. The value of *branding* is and remains dependent on the quality of cattle to be branded.

Freedom

Freedom, "eleutheria" in Greek and "libertas" in Latin, is found in the center of the square. We will, in the coming chapters, examine this more systematically, but here it will be presented briefly.

---

[1] Cicero, De finibus, III, 17, 21. My translation, based on Johannes Sløk's Danish translation in Stoikerne (Berlingske Forlag, 1966, p. 85).

Freedom is not a negative concept. It doesn't involve shaking something off or running away from it; it involves a capacity for confrontation.

But confrontation does not mean frontal attack. Freedom is about confronting something by integrating it. One can only create an inner space of freedom if one constructs it by the norms and ideals that are meaningful in the social reality in which one lives, and if its foundation is a level-headed understanding of what cannot be otherwise.

Freedom is about having the stature to feel joy about all that happens that is beyond our power to control, all that we can neither anticipate nor influence. I don't mean something that happens to others, but that which affects us directly. The stoics used a beautiful word to describe this. They called this spiritual fortitude "eudymia". It is significant that modern man lacks such a concept in his language; we'd rather not accept any of powerlessness.

This tension between the will to shape one's life in the image of the good, on the one hand, and the recognition of necessities, on the other, is the space of freedom. Will must here be understood in relation to ability, and necessity must be understood in both its negative and positive variants. Positive necessity emerges from a regard for the community, while negative necessity emerges from the limits set by nature, technology, knowledge and the unpredictability of events and dynamic processes.

Within this space, freedom can be established as personal autonomy; as "the legislation for one's own life"; as personal autarchy, "to be the cause of one's own life" by making decisive choices oneself; to be the basis for one's own origin (the start of a new life). And freedom can be established by something the Greeks called "ton ef' hemin", i.e., to be the master of one's own house by understanding how to distinguish clearly and soberly between something you can change and something that is beyond your control.

In modernity, the German philosopher Hegel also emphasizes this characteristic of freedom. It is a balance between freedom of action and the recognition of necessity, precisely because he saw it as his mission to conceptualize the foundation of a national community. Some of his thoughts can be used today to rethink the organization as embodying a deeper sense of community than the employment contract invokes—a community that preserves the individual's freedom.

But one thing is certain: freedom has nothing to do with egoism, with taking the law into your own hands, with the right to make your own values, with "going your own way", or with "doing it my way". It

The Greek Square

has nothing to do with narcissism and strategic thoughtlessness. Freedom is something more and different than what you can understand by the concept of "enlightened self-interest". This concept displays a kind of negative freedom that loses itself and fails to be binding because it is finally petty.

Real freedom is about daring to take risking oneself in the serving the interests of others.

If the leader understands this, he will be free.

Chapter 4

The Leader as a Pedagogical Example

The relatively simple premise for bringing in the Greek square as an expression of a normative approach to the problem of creating a new form of leadership and a new organizational methodology is that the leader is to be evaluated according to his virtue and the organization according to its ethos.

As we've already seen in the first chapter, leadership consists in the will and ability to form itself in the image of the good. Leadership is only possible on the basis of a clear concept of self-leadership that can maintain what is distinctive about leadership across all situations and every dynamic context.

This problem is at bottom *pedagogical* but in a broader and more fundamental sense than we otherwise are used to using this concept. The leader should be precisely a pedagogue, both for himself and for others.

The term "pedagogue", which originates from the Greek ideal of education, namely, "paideia", doesn't only allude to the teaching of children, but, more precisely, to lifelong process of learning and the development of a socially relevant formative process. But this learning does not specifically imply merely learning within a technical or professional field; the Greeks called this specified kind of learning "techne", "craft" or "technique", and this occupation did not rank very highly in regard to the acquisition of true knowledge and the actualization of an ethical attitude. During the Roman Period, "paideia" was translated as "humanitas" and became the foundation of a moral and ethical educational ideal whose goal was to create the perfect Roman citizen in combination with the "ancient Roman" and the stoic virtues.

In this sense, pedagogy implies the development of the most responsible approach to the community that is compatible with a regard for oneself as a person from the point of view of eternity.

Like his colleague Seneca, Cicero, who was a philosopher, rhetorician, and senator, buckled under the weight of the confrontation between the moral-ethical attitude and the will to power of the tyrants.

These two men illustrate the profundity of the humanistic ideal. We can find an even more tragic illustration of this opposition with the stoic philosopher Marcus Aurelius, who had the bad fortune of becoming Caesar in 161 A.C.E., a time marked by plague and revolt at the edges of the empire. In his little philosophical masterpiece, called *The Meditations*, we see the clash of morals and power that takes place in the person who has a searching, human soul. Marcus Aurelius would not, as the leader of an empire, accept a compromise with regard to the demands he made of himself as a person. This is a conflict that would not come to an end until he died in 180A.C.E. in the imperial military residence at the river Save near the frontier of the empire.

Such people who have experienced the inner conflicts of leadership assure us that the leader doesn't need to feel alone. Everywhere in the great human comedy and tragedy we call 'history', we find friends, kindred spirits and fellow-sufferers.

But we can also find these people much closer to us, sometimes even within our own organization.

It can sometimes surprise me that even in our time, which is so intently focused on telling stories, so little attention is given to the leader as an example.

This clearly has something to do with the fact that the leader, who must set a proper example of leadership, must have made a decisive break with the autonomy of the manager's role (from the Italian "maneggiara", "to break a horse in", i.e., the person who stands in the middle of the ring and directs the horse by hand). The leader should also be supported by an atmosphere within the organization that is prepared to appropriate the importance of this transformation from manager to leader. But people are all too often inclined to reduce leadership to the "coaching" side of the manager's role without understanding that the leader comprises the whole person. If one is interested in genuine leadership then one must acknowledge that one is a leader also when one executes the manager's often more "technical" functions.

Within an organization where this clarification has occurred, where the leader can stand out as a shining example of normative will and ability – yes, a 'spiritual lighthouse' – the choice of executive candidates and successors will seem much less coincidental and capricious than is the case today. The organization can simply cultivate its own leadership over several generations.

It becomes possible at the same time to convey much more clearly to potential leaders in an organization what it is that is demanded of a leader, and thus what the decision to follow this career path in this context actually involves.

According to Cicero, in his book *De officiis* (*on Duty*), a person's character consists of four components:

- A universal, human character that is characterized by reason, which separates us from the animal.
- An individual, innate character.
- An accidentally acquired character (noble ancestry, royal power, wealth, and influence).
- The character we have chosen and developed ourselves.[2]

Regarding the last component, the result of our self-creation and self-leadership, Cicero says:

But we must first of all decide who and which kind of person we wish to be, and which calling we will follow in life, and this is the most difficult problem of all.[3]

When the organization sets out to decide upon a leader, this is the task that they should be looking for someone to accomplish. It may be accomplished through apprenticeship, through an organizational ethos that promotes normative action, or through internal educational programs that encourage self-management on the road to leadership.

For it is the organization that can promote the spiral motion between good action, on the one hand, and the consciousness of and practical sensitivity for the content of the good and the extent of its interpersonal radicalism.

Aristotle comments on this relationship in the *Nicomachean Ethics*:

on the other hand it appears, there is a state of mind in which a man may do these various [good] acts with the result that he really is a good man: I mean when he does them from choice, and for the sake of the acts themselves.[4]

---

[2] Cicero. *De officiis*, book I, xxx, 107, xxxii 115. Tr. W. Miller. Loeb Edition. London: Harvard University Press 1913/1997.
[3] Ibid. xxxii, 117.
[4] Aristotle. *The Nicomachean Ethics*, VI, xii, 7-8. Tr. H. Rachkham. Loeb Classical Library. London: Harvard University Press, 1926/1994.

The Virtue of Leadership

Here the absence of strategy in good action is emphasized. Conscious choice expresses the state of mind which thoroughly permeates body and soul and which co-exists with a theoretical and practical awareness of the good, which is called *phronesis*. Such a state, which is perceived as personal integrity, autonomy and good will toward others, is the foundation of virtue. We can also call this a "pedagogical attitude" toward oneself and others that concerns learning as much as possible from what happens to you by proving your worth. This pedagogical attitude does not express superiority with regard to professional authority by the person who exercises it. The leader is condemned to be a generalist, i.e., to be a person whose capacities involve having the ability to set a good example, to decide and to motivate. And these abilities should never be fixed within specialized fields of expertise.

In ordinary pedagogical institutions, it is possible for a leader to have an basis in his field even though he may play the part of a generalist, where he is often judged by his efficiency within his area of study by his technical qualifications. But within the private and public sectors, the top leader can't be content to define his position as a generalist through a degree in economics, political science, engineering or law. The generalist is someone you have to constantly work toward becoming, maintaining an open dialogue between many different areas of study. This kind of dialogue can only be balanced by the leader's understanding that the capacity to function as a generalist is proportional to his ability to reflect and act normatively.

Cicero talks about the harmony of reason and instinct in *De finibus* (*on Ends*), and here we could mention the harmony between the various demands that are made of a leader, based on the *hegemony* of the good, which thus presents the possibility for leadership that doesn't accept compromise without pretending that the good and the economical will always be able to be reconciled. The term "hegemony" originates from the stoic *hegemonikon,* which evokes a faculty in the soul that can guide the entire mental and bodily apparatus because it has created itself as a moral-ethical bastion. It does not *exist* in and of itself even though consciousness carries it as a possibility; it is brought into being by the person who allows himself to be guided by the good.

The ability to make us of what happens to you—to fashion yourself in the image of the good (a quality I call *virtue*)—provide us with a basis to elaborate a number of *leadership virtues* with corresponding *social* or *organizational* virtues, as I've done this in my previous books and will also do here. The Danish word for virtue, "dyd", originates from the common Nordic word "dygo" and derives from "du" which is related to "dygtig" (competent) in conjunction with "at du til noget" ("to have a skill"). Virtue, then, doesn't necessarily invoke anything like dull modesty.

In this chapter, however, I'll only cite those virtues that Cicero associates with "humanitas" in relation to the genuine philosophical gentleman. Later, I will work out a systematic catalogue including twelve virtues that characterize true leadership.

Cicero's catalogue of virtues for the philosophical gentleman include:

> *moral and spiritual development, noble-mindedness, dignity and nobility of the human soul; decency, wit, taste, humor, grace, elegance and sensibility; cleverness, politeness and inner balance; kindness, goodness, gentleness, benevolence, hospitality, generosity and magnanimity.*

Two somewhat more concrete virtues also play a role for Cicero, and they are obviously essential for the leader.

In correlation to his consideration of the virtue "decency" ("decorum"), which is a very unobtrusive way to practice the even more essential virtue "integrity" (aequitas), Cicero mentions two Greek virtues, namely *eutaxia* - "modestia" in Latin, "modest" in English, and *eukairia* – "occasio" in Latin.

The first virtue relates to moderation and a restrained style of action. It is seen in the commander-in-chief's composure when structuring a situation, surveying it and maintaining its essential core.

The other virtue relates to punctuality, to convenience, and to timeliness. It expresses a feeling for what the Greeks called *kairios*, "the right moment".

If these virtues can be united in one action, namely, to do the right thing at the right moment, then this is naturally a virtue of leadership *par excellence.*

In part II, I will go into greater depth about what constitutes the foundation of the leader's virtues, his ability to foster organizational legitimacy by expressing personal integrity and decisive well-balanced authority and his relationship to himself or "his self".

PART II

LEADERSHIP AND PERSONAL DEVELOPMENT

Chapter 5

The Self

When you talk about "stepping into character", and when you talk about "choosing yourself", like you do in the tradition of Kierkegaard, this then presupposes a number of very complicated mental structures. The concept of "character" is several thousands of years old and is derived at a theoretical level through philosophical and psychological discourses, and in a manifold of ways in literature. In *Brand*, Ibsen writes:

Don't be one thing today and tomorrow,
and something else in a year.
Be what you are, fully and completely,
And not piecemeal and in parts.

But why not be another a year from now than you are today? Yes, why not be someone other than yourself, a new person? Many dream of just that, and many of our notions about development and learning strive for just such a "new skin". What is it that seems so obviously right in the demand for the permanence of self? Isn't the hypermodern person characterized precisely as a person who wants to "try different roles", as they say: one who is flexible, willing to change, and prepared to put himself on the line?

On the other hand, we often sense that there is "something inside of us" that is "untouchable" or quite simply sacred. The Buddhists speak of this as "atman", something that we cannot master. In this sense, we are all "ring-bearers", "hobbits", that fate has chosen to watch over a force that surpasses our ability to understand it and which we're perpetually tempted to abuse. We are all chosen in this way, without being able to explain it, and inside of us resides a force that can both sustain and destroy. When we feel this way, we often speak of the "self" or the "soul".

In this sense, you know that the character you "step into" when you step into character has always been there. "Become that which you are!" said Marcus Aurelius, emperor and stoic philosopher. Here, character isn't really bound to the social—to the image we have of ourselves and of others—but to something intangible. It constitutes our gifts, our life, and is the secret of "infinity's deceit" or, simply, death – as Søren Kierkegaard called it in the *Concluding Unscientific Postscript*. Emphasizing the importance of cooperation and tolerance across religions, Bill Clinton once said in an interview on Norwegian television, "Most people on this earth believe in an immortal soul that is created by a creator and that will return to him after death." What will return is what we understand as "the self".

It is a precondition in all of the great religions that the "I" constitutes a solid core, something unalterable that we carry with us from birth. Without it, there could be no conscience for it carries a permanent authority with it, so that it would be hard times for morals and ethics in its absence. Conscience is "something" that transcends the "I" and is responsible when I reflect upon "my" actions. This "I" can't simply be its own judge as if it knew everything about itself. It should judge itself on another's behalf, an other it carries inside it, or which it is inside, and which, in the world of religion, has direct access to God or represents him. In Western religion, relatively little is made of the capacity of the "I" to reach the self; it is considered to be a kind of "technique". You can't, on this view, take the last steps on your own; you can take them only with the grace of God. This is not the case in Eastern religions.

From this perspective, stepping into character or choosing oneself wouldn't be the same as identifying oneself with a "social role", but in most cases it would imply leaving it and entering into a state beyond the role. In Western religion this exit, i.e., this departure from one's self, is staged institutionally by the monastic system and in everyday rituals where the priest has the authority to forgive, that is, the authority deliver a person from his self at any given moment. But in modern and in hypermodern society, leaving the role doesn't generally imply moving from one place to another, even though now have many hopefuls who embark on pilgrimages to the gurus of the Far East. Rather, it is a movement that happens on the spot and only occurs in consciousness. We must imagine a transformation in the whole foundation of an attitude: on a more profane basis, we can undertake a rite of passage led by therapists with regard to the individual and by consultants with regard to the organization. This is our great collective illusion about the secular version of something that St. Augustine (a Church Father and the first great philosopher of the Christian religion) called "conversio", our illusion of mental "conversion". But what we turn into is something that is discretely located somewhere between vague conceptions of an enhanced "quality of life" and an enhanced ability to optimize. The bungee-jump replaces the leap of faith along with the inverted crucifixion, guaranteeing that the speed at which the mind develops will on the whole correspond to the familiar pace of "technological" change. In a two-fold sense, we are "busying ourselves".

Ever since Plato determined that thought is the soul's conversation with itself, philosophy, religion and psychology have governed our inner universe, which involves at least two interlocutors: the "I" and the "me". Their relationship to each other is called "reflection". They mirror one another and can switch roles. Even the relationship here is crucial, as Søren Kierkegaard emphasized, and the particular relationship that is established between the "I" and the "me" characterizes a person's philosophy of life. Conscience is found in the tension between these two poles, even though their reciprocal dialogue seems to be monitored by a third thing (by the self). Thus the possibility of our acting morally and ethically is here legitimatized. But it also makes it possible for us to act rationally, to "reflect upon our actions", just as we project the same figure into another person when we seek to understand him or her. We spontaneously appeal to the fact that the other can have other designs on himself when dealing with me.

Certain philosophers, sociologists and psychologists claim that this I-me relationship is merely an internalization of our early relationships with those who raised us, or that it is an automatic way to confirm the power that the group has over us. But it is a fact that the soul talks to itself and that what it talks to itself about is in particular is who it is that is speaking "in there".

The German romantic philosopher Schelling went so far as to assert that a person chose his self before the dawn of time, before the beginning of the world; indeed, at the same time that God created the world.

But there are alternatives.

In contrast to this Christian conception of a self, which is identical with our immortal soul and which separates itself from the I and the me (which in turn are the result of both socialization and our personal life stories, of right and wrong choices), stands the edifice of Greek thought, which has been resurrected in postmodernism, as seen in the works of philosophers such as Michael Foucault and Gilles Deleuze. It claims that I am nothing substantial in advance, but that I am something that comes into existence because I take upon myself the enterprise of creating myself. There is an unmistakable resonance of stoicism in this message.

To have the ability to create myself implies that acting ethically or morally becomes even more urgent because it is only through this ability that I can build the foundation upon which the self is represented. In the *Nicomachean Ethics,* Aristotle maintains the paradox when he asserts that I can only can do (the) good after I know what the good is, but that I can know what the good is when I have had experience doing it. (This paradox will be familiar to leaders who know that I can only lead when I know what good leadership is, but to know what good leadership is leadership experience).

Stepping into character here means becoming conscious of the line one has chosen to follow through life and then holding to it without compromise. Thus, little by little, you become the person you ought to be – or owe it to yourself to become. To desire and to do the good can be understood as a diet, or like a cure for a disease: "Cure your life!" proclaimed Epicurus. The pill ("pharmakon") that was ingested then was philosophy. Becoming a person who can take his life upon himself and show himself worthy of the event takes time and demands patience.

Christianity emphasizes the importance of revelation in the quest to reach our true selves. We must believe in "the word". The religions of the East emphasize the hard road of meditation. The therapeutic movements of the West, especially Jungian psychology, stresses that we can find our way into this self through contemplation guided therapy, e.g., by analyzing the messages that our dreams supply us with about ourselves.

On the other hand, the Greeks and the postmodernists emphasise the idea that we can create ourselves. This is also seen in the term *ethos*, and with the long "e" (the "eta") "ethos" means "character", "the potential given us at birth" and even "home town". "Ethos" is not necessarily a core in a person; it is a potential. But we can only become conscious of this potential through "ethos" with the short "e" ("epsilon"), which denotes good habits, the mark one leaves on one's own self. But this ability to stamp out one's own coinage, the capacity for goodness, is only possible if it is fortified through upbringing. In this setting, character can be "created", *poiesis*. To choose one's self is an *etho-poietical* process—a process of "self-creation" where we build ourselves up through our good deeds until we mold a solid core. But this build-up, this "edification", only can only happen on a background of stable norms, and it takes imagination to be able to interpret situations based on the good, just as it demands improvisation if one is not to fall back into being a stickler for the rules. It is like learning to play an instrument. The more you practice, the more you can refine your expression and concentrate on the details without losing sight of the whole.

All tendencies within Greek philosophy emphasize the importance of the social, the community.

Christianity seizes upon "the word", while the Greek mind focuses on the norms of society. But from both sides we are given the opportunity to become ourselves within the social context, whether through Bible study, sermons and the church or through the education "academies" (paideia) of our choice.

The problem now, as already mentioned, is that the meaning of "stepping into character" and "choosing oneself" both seem to be processes where you meet yourself by stepping out of the social, i.e. "the superficial sociality". Socrates let himself be executed because he despised the popular tyrants. Christ died because he wouldn't share the opinions of the Pharisees. Kierkegaard looked beyond the tame and civil version of Christianity. Ibsen's heroes sought beyond the predetermined bourgeois paths of social success.

But can the leader seek himself in a truer community, somehow hidden behind the superficial one?

Isn't rather that to step into character and to choose yourself depends upon an extremely limited set of possibilities for action, which do not involve roles such as marketing manager or vice president, but rather roles like "integrity" and "honesty"?

Or can a person step into character "within" any social activity: as a piccolo, an elite soldier and as a management consultant?

If so, then this involves applying principles that allow us to become one with this self, which either makes any functional expression unimportant – following the motto: "Deep down, I am a Christian." Or it involves having psychological functional criteria for all social roles in order to achieve success, which then depends on living out the role as fully as possible, and which leads to stepping into character, to choosing yourself.

But both of these amount to the suggestion that all of the differentiations of role functions, which are always being constructed in modern society, can somehow be "fitted" into the "eternal person" within us.

In this sense, you could be entirely focused on the bottom line, beyond soft values and human consideration and still step into character. Or, you could admit that you couldn't live up to a role and then simply step into character through this "honesty". In the first instance, you have an "I" that is a "survivor". In the other instance, you have an "I" that is a "loser". But both are equally and wholly a self.

Let us now get still more systematic in this discussion with the aim of concluding it.

Ever since David Hume wrote about the difficulties of determining identity during the 18th century, philosophical discourse has been aware of the problem of explaining how a person can simultaneously possess a core and yet still change. For what is it that constitutes the core? If it is the body, then the cells regenerate completely every seven years. If it is the reflective consciousness, i.e., our personal relationship between the "I" and "me", then it has no tangible form but consists of a "sense of something" in a state of mind or in an "inner attitude".

The question here is, what is it that allows me to say that I experience something that happens to *me* as something that happens to "the same person"?

On the other hand, thinking that we simply refashion ourselves every time we face a new event is strange to us. Wouldn't most people, including most of the philosophers, say that it is our personal memory that affords us a feeling of uniqueness? To be sure, no one person's memories resemble another's exactly – partly because no one experiences precisely the same thing, and partly because no two people interpret something from a shared experience in the same way.

Søren Kierkegaard was also very conscious of the importance of the correlation is between identity and memories.

In *Stages on Life's Way* he writes:

> *The recollected is not, like the remembered, indifferent to memory, indifferent to recollection. You can throw the recollected away, but like Thor's hammer it comes back. And not just like that: it has a longing after recollection like a dove, yes, like a dove that, however often it is sold, can never belong to anyone else ...*

But the question now is: Am I only the sum of my memories, their particular pattern; do they create me, and am I me because I have them, or are they mine because I am something more?

Most of us would tend to answer yes to the last question. Even the postmodern philosophers who talk about an anonymous "I", i.e., that identity is a "user illusion", and who focus on the "process" inherent in all identities, would not reject the existence of some form of consistency in us. It is in any case certain that we cannot logically refer to change, much less to transformation, if consistency doesn't exist, if there is no "something" that undergoes change and transformation. There is no journey if nobody travels.

These two conceptual constructs, "to step into character" and to "choose yourself", which I have already mentioned and which are essential to hypermodern management, can now be given a more precise meaning, one that sets them at a distance the ideas expounded by new-age ideologists.

If we distinguish between "being that which I expect of myself" and "being that which others expect of me" and finally "being that which the role expects of me" then stepping into character and choosing myself places the main emphasis on the first dimension. It concerns my relationship to myself.

But these concepts have great social significance because the modification of my self has to, in some way or another, succeed in practice.

Therefore, we have to make a distinction that maintains one pole where you can almost invisibly step into character for yourself and one pole where you very distinctly step into character for others and in relation to a role. In this last instance, "the choosing myself" implies a change in my social conduct.

In almost all cases, it is clearly expected that both stepping into character and choosing yourself should lead to being taken more seriously as a leader. There is a "therapeutic" element in these processes, and we should bear in mind that "therapeuo" in Greek originally denotes helping someone to help himself.

But at the same time we can also imagine that a person steps into character or chooses himself "for his inner man", as Luther said. If you're a tailor, you cut with the same precision and stitch with the same accuracy as before you stepped or chose. No change will be noticed by your wife, your children or your dog.

But in hypermodern society, where interviews have shown that most young people in the job market, regardless of whether they're students or sales clerks, want jobs that develop them as people, it is very difficult to imagine stepping into character or choosing yourself without it influencing the conduct that you display at work or in other social relationships.

Much further down the road, these concepts will come to mean that you can reconcile yourself with your own existence. You begin to better appreciate those you associate with – or you begin to choose to make do without particular people. You'll demand more from your work. You'll work with a greater sense of commitment. You'll assume your role, and as a boss, you'll become "fiercer" or "gentler" than you dared to be before.

What is crucial in this discussion, however, is that a distinction must be maintained between personal development beyond or in contrast to the social and a development that unfolds in accordance with this. We have to acknowledge this dilemma. If not for other reasons, then because there exists a range of job activities and a range of social relations that can be which cannot set human potential free.

When we are aware of this we can then, to a higher degree, also focus on those social roles and relations that actually make it possible to step into character and choose ourselves.

As the reader has perhaps already guessed, I think that coaching should have the function precisely of maintaining this dilemma. It shouldn't be about locating the blame for problems at work in the individual's psychological constitution.

Chapter 6

To Step into Character

If the leader's role were unambiguous, then there wouldn't be any problem here. But leadership is a vague phenomenon. Leaders can be many things because many objective and subjective expectations are found regarding the role of leadership.

Plato's idea of the leader as a paternal, omniscient "shepherd" makes clear sense of how you step onto character by choosing yourself as a 100% responsible and moral person who can and will find support in the hierarchically constructed authority of the position. Here, one's eternal "human nature" is combined with the temporal demands of the role—even in the details—because it is simply one's self who has responsibility. In principle, you do everything for the good of the community and *never* prioritize yourself, even though this by no means rules out dilemmas and a troubled conscience when you have to break the golden rule for the sake of the survival of the organization—or when you have to dismiss your employees or have to weaken your competitors or wipe them out. Still, such a patriarchal figure of leadership may well constitute a space for leadership, one that makes it easier to lead, because the relevant course of action is found within a permanent framework—regardless of whether it even begins to provide platform for modern and effective leadership. In one way or another, power and morals become "natural" companions, even if this offends our sensibilities.

But at every level of leadership that we find in organizations today, stepping into character is easier said than done.

A sales manager who seriously compares his product with his competitors' can easily come to feel that he's deceiving the customers when he asserts that his product is very much better than the others'. A financial manager who takes a loan that is the most advantageous for the company might know that the money he is borrowing comes from a place that doesn't live up to his idea of good business.

In both cases we might be shocked to hear that stepping into character means that the sales manager should exaggerate and the financial manager should invoke the slogan "non olet", i.e., that "money does not smell". It's evident that stepping into character and choosing yourself can only occur on the basis of a commonly accepted moral code—a code that is carefully adjusted in relationship to our idea of the good.

This can vary in the details, but it follows the so-called golden rule: Do onto others as you would have them do onto you.

If the center is the source of power over other people, then any talk of stepping into character and about choosing yourself in relation to the role of the leader has to depend upon the practical subjection of this power to a moral or ethical assessment.

This can mean that we have to place ourselves above what "others may expect of me when I have to be that which I am".

In this context, then, stepping into character and choosing yourself must mean comporting yourself such that you can better honor those demands that you in part make of yourself as a moral person and in part relegate to the role where these moral and ethical demands should be honored.

But this relationship is much more complicated than it immediately seems.

If I am to step into character as a personnel manager, for example, i.e., if I am to change or intensify my performance in this field, should I work on my authority or strengthen my sense of sympathy? Here another difficult element is brought into the discussion: the fact that I cannot step into character or choose myself unless this is done on the basis of an interpretation of concrete situations and is based on an intelligent assessment of the people involved—a relationship that is at the same time quite dependent on the availability of relevant and adequate information.

It is a widespread and unfortunate illusion that you can step into character once and for all. On the contrary: it demands hard work, *askesis*, day in and day out.

In this sense, stepping into character, choosing yourself, demands not only that I come to terms with myself, but that I come to terms also with the situation and its context, including the people it contains. In short, it demands *empathy*.

But empathy isn't a simple phenomenon. It has its strategic aspects. It is one thing to understand the internal state of another's I-me relationship, to take another's mental temperature. It is quite another to determine the consequences that should be drawn from this.

Should I be gentle and yielding toward an ineffectual employee? Or should I be stern, thus strengthening his relationship to himself by giving him clear parameters to "work" with?

If I am going to try to break a cocky know-it-all, then I have to be sure that it is not just a façade. And even if it is a façade, should I break him down anyway? Is this, then, in other words, what it means to step into character here—that I, as a leader, should make full use of my power and authority?

Here, there are actually only two alternatives to psychological plans of action: empathetic intuition or practical wisdom. In principle, the first is just a side of the second, and one thing is certain: these plans of action, understood as methods of evaluation, cannot be learned in courses or classes, and they can't be acquired through any kind of conversion or rapture, or the doggedly serious confessions resulting from this. Ethics and morals can't be administered like silicone.

Whatever the individual might have in the way of personal and moral resources, however, the actualization of them isn't anything we can anticipate in private; to a certain degree, they are only things to improve upon. This demands not only practicing the act of stepping into character or "daring to be yourself" among other people, but it depends on something else—something decisive—namely the specific character of the *situation* in which it occurs.

A situation that in its content and its context possesses a form that is capable of establishing the meaningful background against which to step into character or choose your self is called an *event*.

Here I don't mean by this that the background of events themselves cannot be established by routine, i.e., the structured and rehearsed entourage of situations. Stepping into character, however, is all about being able to break with routine. The role of the leader is associated with certain types of situation and with particular actions, which can offer "exemplary" or even "epochal" events, where the individual can demonstrate his abilities and will have to fill out the role with his entire personality—as a lesson to ponder, both for himself and for others.

I have to mention here that that I'm not necessarily alluding to the individual actualizing his "self". The self is an entity that doesn't need to be brought into this context, because what's really at stake here is the *relationship* that I have to myself. Echoing philosophers like Aristotle and Kant, you could say that stepping into character or choosing yourself results in an inner concordance or inner *harmony* between I and me. These two philosophers employ/apply one of these concepts each. Aristotle talks of "single-mindedness" while Kant invokes an inner "accord" (a musical metaphor) with oneself.

But the relationship gets complicated once again—because we're not talking about events within the realm of intimacy, in private life, but about organizational, strategically circumscribed events. In this context, consideration of the company and its solidarity/fellowship *must* play an important role.

To step into character implies both actualizing your own moral and human potential and serving the cause of the organization.

The problem is that these two entities can often stand in opposition to one another.

In general, the problems that we've touched upon can be expressed as a dilemma regarding the leader's opportunities for stepping into character and choosing himself.

Some organizational events can almost dissolve this dilemma allowing a fusion of the role and the person, but in many cases and on many levels of leadership, these two (the person and the role) are and remain incompatible with one another because the business world is subject to a technical-economical rational objective that doesn't to the same extent govern our choices within the sphere of intimacy. An example of this fusion is that of the leader who summons his employees to an extraordinary meeting during a time when the company's state of the company seems unstable, and where the employees enter the meeting expecting a pep talk—or worse. But instead, the leader opens the door, and the employees stand in front of a well-decked table. He now begins by complimenting each employee for his or her extraordinary efforts in such a trying time. And he finishes off by announcing a bonus. This is a true story.

In general, it is all about preserving character of leadership as a dilemma, and about not imagining that these dilemmas can be resolved through a general fusion of economy and morals or of humanity and management. In a positive sense, the leader has to convey to the employee that they're in the same boat, without making them accomplices.

But let us look a little more closely at how we experience other people, and how other people experience us.

PART III

ORGANIZATION AND THE OTHER

Chapter 7

The Social and the Event

One could be inclined to believe in taking the kind of philosophy that is represented by Kierkegaard, that is, existential philosophy, as a point of departure, one will automatically set the individual before the community, and do this to such a degree that any understanding of the social will itself have to proceed from the individual. In this sense, and in order to make a successful life possible, the individual person should be able to find within himself the ground of experience, thought, judgment, and life itself.

This is of course in every way an illusion. We aren't merely condemned to be with others, as Sartre said; we are created from that "otherness" we call "the social". This means that even though we're creatures of nature, this nature is formed by the communities we encounter throughout our childhood and upbringing, as well as in our adult lives. And if we are to find ourselves as individuals, this will happen as we embrace concepts that are given to us by this community. Just as nobody is able to create his own language, nobody can consider his own disposition without anticipating the norms and perspectives, the criteria and objectives through which this nature has been filtered through thousands of years.

Nevertheless, nature seems sometimes to break through its social enclosure, just as something else can seem to seep in through the social, something that is more than first nature (our animal nature) and our second nature (our social identity).

The other person, then, is revealed to us in a great variation between two extremes. In the first extreme, the other is a purely an object, purely a means. And the best illustration of this extreme appears where the other is conceived of solely as meat, that is, food—whether this is attributed to bitter necessity or some other inclination. At the opposite extreme the other is a bearer of the divine. We recognize this mode of thought from the figure of Christ or from the notion of "shekinah", the halo that surrounds the divine person according to the tradition of medieval Jewish mysticism. In the previous century, the French-Jewish thinker, Emmanuel Lévinas, applied and developed this line of thinking further. He believed that each person who stands before us is the potential carrier of the divine by virtue of his face. The face is able to guard itself against reduction to the flesh or to a symbol (like the racist pictures depicting Jews with faces that resemble rats, but also like the depiction of the face as an icon or idol, as in the propaganda posters of Stalin and Mao that once hung on every street corner, or like the portraits of Hitler and Mussolini, which could be found in every classroom and every public office). The face somehow manages to remain inviolate and thus affords a foundation for all ethics.

But let us look briefly at the first extreme: the other as food. This can be seen in an example originating from an article by the anthropologist Kennet Pederson entitled "Ist der Mensch was er isst?", which relates the French Huguenot Jean de Léry's account in *A history of a voyage to the land of Brazil* from 1578. Léry escaped from The Massacre of St. Bartholomew on August 24, 1572, and participated in the French attempt to colonize Brazil. Here, he encountered the Tupi Indians, who ate their enemies. Importantly, they did so only after the Tupi had treated them decently for awhile, fattening them up and appointing them to the positions people's occupied by members of the tribe that had fallen in the war. They would become heads of families, blacksmiths, etc. The primitives here had an excuse, namely, their primitiveness. At roughly the same time in France, however, after a pogrom, the Catholics, disciples of Christ, fried and sold the hearts and livers of the Huguenots in the butcher stands at the foot of the church.

In South America, it was common custom to be offered a forearm, served well done. In Christendom this was hardly an acceptable action. But the Christians nevertheless eat each other when they really 'cut loose', remarks Jean de Léry. And not only that, on Sundays, behind the closed doors of their religious institutions, they would eat their god. In his remarks on the Catholics, Léry mentions that you don't have to go to America to find cannibals. Léry also comments on the Catholics' relationship to the Eucharist. He notes:

> *(They were stubborn on this point). And this to such a degree that, without knowing how it was possible, not only would they eat the blood of Jesus Christ concretely, as opposed to spiritually, but what's worse is how they would chew and swallow it completely raw, just like the savages...*

Is it this deep-seeded cultural metaphor for unification that resides beneath our dreams and the dreams of philosophy to reach all the way into the other person? Stronger than a touch, a good deed, a conversation, yes, stronger than a kiss, stronger than coitus, stronger than the mixed blood of a child, it seems, is the desire to consume your enemy, your ancestor, your child and your god; to edify yourself on his power.

This is indeed extreme, but it touches on our other extreme, the divinity of man. There is obviously a quite gradual transition from our average experience of the other on an everyday basis to our will to confront the divine. This graduation is conveyed by social roles and social positions, yet also by something that the sociologist Max Weber called "charisma", from the Greek term "chara", meaning "grace", "joy" and "kindness". Charisma is a quality that a person may possess that brings him or her closer to the qualities that characterize the divine. We know of this at once spontaneous and staged apotheosis of human beings from our beliefs in the healing powers of the king's garments, indeed, of the king's gaze or of the Pope's cloak, which is only a thing of the past in a partial sense. How much did Elvis' shoes cost at Sotheby's? The concept of a "saint", which plays a crucial role for millions of Catholics to this day, is a way in which we convert an inclination into an institution. We recognize that certain people manifest behaviour that places them somewhere between the human and the divine.

In between these extremes, somewhere between the cannibal and the saint, the "average person" resides, and it is also here that we meet the leader.

The complex spiritual or cultural movement that we call "humanism" takes the fact that behind all faces and within all bodies there exists a fundamental and uniform human nature as point of departure. This does not exclude variety and difference but rather gives it a space in which to flourish.

Throughout the last 500 years, a crucial part of this humanism has consisted in teaching people to filter each other out of the social roles that have formed the foundation for positions of power and privilege: positions that have elevated them above the evaluation of their actions and intentions, which is the right of 'everyman' to contribute to.

An enormously important factor in this evolution is the creation of a *formative process*—the shaping of an apparatus of historical dispositions, of moral integrity, of philosophical experience, and of the ability to exercise reason—all of which makes *empathy* possible. Empathy has two sides. It includes the ability to break down the emotional barrier between you and your subordinate *and* the corresponding ability to break down the emotional barrier between you and your superior.

Empathy is both protective and critical. In the first instance, you'd say, "He is also human," while in the second instance you'd say, "He is only human."

It is worth noting that empathy presupposes certain social conditions. In a state society empathy becomes identical with institutionalized charity or with mercy that is marked by strategic beneficence— even though in certain instances it is also diminished by generous sympathy—while sympathy in a democratic society actually almost expresses both a right of the person who receives it and a duty of the person who practices it.

Empathy rests on the golden rule: "Do not do onto others and what's theirs what you do not want them to do onto you and what's yours!"

Historically, empathy has been approximated through legislation, including the preventive legislation in the 1800s regarding the length of the workday and working conditions, regarding the perception of crime and the treatment of criminals, regarding the conventions for acceptable behavior in war, the demand for general education and a minimum standard of living. The emergence of the welfare state in certain European countries after the Second World War established empathy as a system in a national framework.

All totalitarian regimes partially suspend the spontaneous force of empathy in our emotional lives through legislation and the system of justice, but on a larger scale these regimes remove empathy, either by decreeing that certain groups of citizens are either not "normal people" or by placing them outside of the legislation that applies to all "law-abiding" citizens. We don't need to torment ourselves by recalling the previous century's equanimity in this context. Instead we'll focus on democracies or on societies that at least contain a modicum of democratic procedures and the institutions that give them the right to suspend empathy. This, of course, applies to the military and to the police, but it has applied especially to the firm, and still does.

For when a person sells his labour power, he to a certain degree surrenders his right to receive empathy, and in so far as this occurs in particular hierarchies of leadership, he also casts off his obligation to feel empathy for others. The existence of the unions can be attributed to this relationship: the right to receive empathy "vertically" and to receive and exercise it "horizontally" (as tangible solidarity) should be taken by force or practiced in secret. Industrialism can be seen as the history of a slow and meticulous devouring of people, where the bodies were consumed through cleverly devised, gradual mechanisms of dissolution, called "division of labour" and "factory work".

What was created in companies was something the stoics called an "adiaphoristic" field—an area where existing moral customs and ethics do not apply, and need not be practiced. Here, people aren't judged by their general humanity, but by their ability and will to live up to the demand that is specified by that role that they fill. Some are fodder for the machines, while others control them.

It is curious, but finally logical, that the predominant arguments presented to disqualify empathy are always deployed in reference to the optimization the individual's utility, i.e., the quality of life under given circumstances—as well as its being the result of the individual's free choice. Regardless of whether you are eaten, prepare the meal or consume it, it is invariably claimed that you chose to sell your labour and actually desired the working conditions presented to you and in which you are absorbed. Hard-handed and one-sided leadership is praised for promoting efficiency. The piece-work system, which the labour movement accepted, seems on the surface long thought to have given only a tiny space for the worker's personal initiative and ingenuity. Today, the 50 to 70 year-old participants in the consumer paradise from the 1960s and 1970s are paying the price: a ruined body.

Aside from the paradoxical element in this type of argument, it illustrates that the precondition for empathy, both when it is practiced and when it is suspended, is that the individual is given a free choice. Empathy cannot be forced upon us, neither in receiving empathy or in giving it—though it can often feel that way.

The construal of freedom as the basis of empathy illustrates the model of consciousness that empathy is generally built upon. Consciousness, on this view, is governed by a superior authority that can survey the actions that the individual undertakes. We call this authority "conscience", and often perceive it as a kind of moral authority or simply as a "moral instinct", though we sometimes forget that it presumes an ability to be self-conscious, to be reflective. Greek thought revealed early on that the moral sense is a result of personal effort, but it is an effort that emerges from a voluntary desire to become a decent person.

Christianity, however, abolished free choice or, rather, it cast it thoroughly into confusion by invoking "original sin", so that we must choose the good in contrast to our nature in order to be delivered from it. Christianity made the good deed a necessity for the salvation of the soul, a necessary evil that seems to conjure up an image of renunciation, instead of providing a ground upon which to dare the notion that the person who really and truly desires the good will perfect his nature. In this sense, Christianity transformed the most important act between people (an act that originates from the need to want the best for another) into something strategic or something trivial (a duty to "thy neighbor"). The ethical or moral fantasy, which rests on an objective ability to evaluate people and situations, is banished from the territory of the good because goodness is systemized through stereotypical acts of duty. The Danish author, Johannes V. Jensen's wonderful short story, "Bakmandens Hund", can be mentioned in passing as a study in ethical fantasy and savoir faire beyond all piety, because the hero consciously loses a game in which he bets something very valuable against something apparently worthless, a dog, in order to be able to secretly give to another a very large, very charitable gift.

The point here is that doing good demands fostering/cultivating within oneself a social intelligence, which depends on/presupposes tact, generosity, and modesty.

In this sense empathy doesn't merely result from a demand; it becomes an art. We can learn this from the stoics. That's why they reject pity—because it doesn't express respect for that person to whom you offer this sentiment.

Today, empathy has become an important element in the range of competences which is demanded from the new type of leader. The leader has to be able to coach—both his colleagues and his subordinates—while coaching of superiors hardly exists—and he has to be able to receive coaching as well. The leader should also be prepared to enter into a kind of mentor relationship where by his courteousness affords him the opportunity to enrich his own experience of reality by contact with other leaders from other corporations or worlds. Both parties naturally profit from this, especially the elder leader who, through his role as mentor, can suddenly put his experiences into words.

The Greek name, "Mentor", which refers to the character in *The Odyssey*, has a basis of meaning that arises from the events in the story. *The Odyssey* ends with Ulysses finally returning home.[5] When he does, he has to get throw out the suitor who is laying claim to his estate and his wife. He receives the aid of his son, Telemachos, an old pig farmer, and that of an exceedingly old and decrepit man named Mentor, who is a philosopher and Telemachos' former teacher. In order for Mentor's help to be effective, the goddess Athena, who is Ulys-

---

[5] The concept of Mentor has been widely used through the best seller *Aventures de Télémaque* by Fénelon from 1699.

ses' protector, possesses him. Because of this, Mentor can hurl the large spear with deadly force.

In other words, Mentor is a very old man who, by virtue of the grace of destiny, again becomes a warrior.

Like Mentor, the leader can thus carry his spear without shame.

Now, it is probably quite obvious that the introduction of empathy into a context from which it is legally and practically excluded, i.e., the modern corporation, can be grounded in reasons beyond fact that culture has become more democratic, or that (some) people have won greater equality in matters of knowledge and competence, or that the concept of justice has to a degree become the foundation for the entirety of our social lives.

Beyond these reasons, empathy has become important because management is forced to give the individual employee increased liberty—in part because management can no longer mandate work in its details, and in part because it is dependent on the employees' cooperation regarding the quality of the product and the potential for innovation. Moreover, the present shifting of the balance within the job market in favor of the workforce. The demand for qualified workers already surpasses its supply of them. This observation also seems to apply to the demand for suitable leaders. What is now in short supply are qualified employees *and* qualified leaders. This places totally new demands on leadership and organizational initiatives. Even among the most ephemeral nuances, power can no longer suspend the employees' right to be met on the premises of their whole humanity. The other side of this coin is that power has to be imported into the employee himself, as the epitome of the demands he now makes of himself. The employee must see himself as if he were another, namely, the leader.

Chapter 8

Experiencing the Other

What follows is a brief survey of certain important philosophical theories about the experience of the other. It should be emphasized, however, that only the last of these theories involve the most essential aspect, namely, the event in which our experience of the other happens.

We can divide these theories into three kinds.

1. Those that conceive of the other as a riddle that should be solved, or a secret to be kept.

2. Those that conceive of the other as something that is already contained in the way one relates to oneself through the articulation of feelings and through the use of language—and can therefore be anticipated.

3. Those that conceive of the relationship to the other as generated through a third element: the meeting or the event.

All of these three types of theories of course contain a little of the universe proper to the others. It should also be emphasized that only few select theories are chosen, and this choice does not imply an assessment of the merits of the ones that have been left on the side.

All these theories inquire into the possibility of empathy in general in the form the epistemological question about the possibility of "seeing what's behind another's face". In addition to this, they share the idea that there is an attitude that serves as a supplement to empathy, namely, the ability to see oneself from outside, i.e., the ability to see yourself through the eyes of another. This 'other' will generally appear as what Adam Smith called "the impartial observer" in *The Theory of Moral Sentiments* and which sociologists have more recently called "the generalized other", following George Herbert Mead. Although Smith's definition is overtly stoic, since he emphasizes that the impartial observer's neutrality originates from the relationship in which he represents the moral norm, both of these perspectives maintain that our conscience always has something about it that lies above and beyond the personal. The judgment we can pass upon ourselves by sensing ourselves through our actions is at all times determined by the moral substance of the community.

On this foundation the philosophers of course ask whether or not conscience merely consists in the judgment of others, and in being judged in general, as something that resides in our consciousness as a kind of list of criteria that makes its appearance through an active illusion and is experienced as an "authority", namely, as the "voice of conscience". These types of arguments will often be substantiated by asserting that a child who grows up alone in the wilderness will have no sense of morality. Opponents of this view, then, say that the sense of morality is built into consciousness in the form of disposition for conscience.

This discussion is relatively fruitless, but the discussion regarding the relationship between a personal and social morality is not.

Whether a person has the right to think on his own behalf, to proceed on the basis of his personal standards, is a part of the central problem that concerns us here, that is, the problem of whether we can understand each other at all. Is moral autonomy an illusion that arises from the failure to appreciate concepts that on the face of it merely mean different things? The question is valid: how can we know that empathy isn't just a projection, or a question of the failure to appreciate the omnipotence of language? And how can we know that the other does not think and feel completely differently than we imagine?

It is the last area where the modern philosophers begin—with language as the basis of our having a shared reality that reciprocally concerns our "inner space". The ability to speak itself presupposes that we can ascribe a real existence to one another's feelings and thoughts, and not merely experience them as something we dream or invent. But since languages are tied to different cultures, the reality that these different cultures presuppose of each other isn't necessarily the same. Before the 1800s, most people who undertook to consider our relationships to each other would have assumed that all civilized people feel and think in the same way. Paradoxically, the closer we come to one another on a daily basis (not only because of the population growing each day) the greater is the mystery that we become to one another. One can explain, though maybe not understand (let alone accept), that the enlightened people of 18th century Europe could pose questions about whether the Indians, who began appearing in Europe as trophies brought home from the colonies, were actually people at all. But one may rightly wonder why communication in general should be made into a problem, and not just where it is a "natural" result of different cultural values or entirely different experiences.

It is also evident that in this age of globalization, it will no longer be theories that perceive the other as a mystery that will dominate the picture. On the contrary, the old question concerning the practical possibility of empathy will be raised anew. And it will be asked in relation to the question of the opportunities we have to form ourselves in such a way that we can live up to the responsibilities we have to other people, regardless of skin color, belief or class. We live under the conditions of unlimited travel that Immanuel Kant already envisaged in his work *Perpetual Peace* from 1795 (*Zum ewigen Frieden. Ein philosophischer Entwurf*), which we will return to in Part IV.

The arguments for this new "ethical" wave will either be of the type that David Hume already presented in the 1750s, namely, that a concern for the utility of society demands a set of social virtues be entrenched around our central capacity for empathy, or of the type that Adam Smith contended, namely, that it is the concern for our own happiness that depends on this entrenchment. This, of course, does not mean that all ethics can be supported, or ever is supported, by functionalistic arguments, which show that an ethical action is that action which is ultimately the most rational because it promotes the greatest happiness for the greatest amount of people, or show that businesses that have high moral standards also have the most stable stock values, or show that ethically substantiated action is the least inconsistent with the realisation of enlightened self-interests. But it would be a great misunderstanding to underestimate the role of such arguments in the effort to establish a world community. Even if one attends to the environment in order to make money, and even though one sells medicine at a low price to developing countries in order to be on good terms with the regimes and create potential customers for other products, the environment *is* protected and people *are* given access to medicine. Taking a broader view, and looking at matters in a larger time frame, it is very difficult to reject the prospect of placing ideals or norms that apply to everyone into a functionalistic context. The negative discrimination of others only results in getting what one wants if one has enough power. Culturally limited norms, on the other hand, often lose their functionality when they're seen as potentially general norms—hence the threat from religions that want their rituals and more specific sides of their view of human nature to become global.

There is, in reality, no need to tie functionality to utility or happiness; one can instead arrive at fundamental concepts for a fully actualized human existence—concepts like freedom, justice, beauty, truth and goodness, i.e., those ideals that ideally govern Western culture, and which I have included in the Greek square—and stop there. These types of concepts obviously require interpretation, and this make them not unlike concepts such as "usefulness" and "happiness", which are also open to interpretation and are also bound to the breadth of one's chosen perspective. It is true that some people occasionally try to quantify them; but by doing this they only kid themselves, and us, into thinking that they are precise. But to understand the last set of concepts presupposes understanding the first set, not the other way round.

All things considered, these reflections are nothing other than a way of questioning the ground upon which the concept of function itself rests. The concepts of freedom, justice, beauty, truth and goodness are ways of scotching the wheel of culture; they can easily support themselves as foundational, irreducible 'values'. But they are also the cornerstones in the foundation of a human existence that doesn't merely meet the demands of a set of minimum requirements but ultimately strives for the full development of every human being as the only valid perspective on our economic situation. These concepts are, in other words, "ideal", "normative" and "utopian".

Let us now turn to the three mentioned conceptions of the possibility of experiencing the other. It will become clear that we are here not just dealing with an interesting philosophical exercise, but with a set of problems see from a variety of angles that pertain to the relationship that the leader can, and perhaps *ought*, to have to the individual and to the organization.

1. The Other as a riddle or a mystery
If the other is a stranger, it can be by virtue of both his power and his powerlessness. In both instances we are dependent on him, but in different ways. It is important, however, that in both instances we can immunize his strangeness by bringing him into our community. Ideally we can do this by convincing him that if he's strong, his strength is dependent on our weakness. Or if he is weak, then his weakness can indict our strength. The German philosopher G.W.F. Hegel called this complicated game *recognition*.

Recognition plays an enormous role in the modern organization, both when it is given and when it is received by the leader. But Hegel's point is that recognition cannot be displayed unless there's a third element that both partners can refer to. This third element is their sense of community, which Hegel described as the "objective spirit", and can easily be made sense of in the modern organization through concepts such as "atmosphere", "climate", or "culture", and especially "ethos", i.e., "spirit".

Oppositions between people based on power or on advantages that are grounded in differences of knowledge, competence, resources, experience, personality, etc., can only be accepted without loss of legitimacy as long as they exists in relation to the acceptance of a common cause. The individual has to find them fair because they serve a function. In another context, the differences might be experienced as inhibiting and unjustifiable relics of history, as atavisms. Older employees with experience and education can only tolerate a younger boss if they get a sense that he is actually *capable* of something that is necessary in order for the organization to survive. Conversely, an engineer can work on equal terms with a semi-skilled worker in the context of one of the company's particular projects, and then return to his role of middle manager when the project is completed. The wage level that top executives receive abroad may seem incomprehensible to Danes because the seven or eight figure salaries don't seem to correspond to the possible performance of any individual. On the other hand, those who are elevated within the hierarchy choose to give up bonuses if the company is hard-pressed, as long as their efforts are registered in one way or another. On the whole, people can demonstrate enormous tolerance of each other's differences as soon as it is legitimized in the name of the community the individuals who deserve it. The quick-witted and ambitious employee is able restrain himself in front of his slow-but-steady colleague because at the end of the day he *has* to work with him, even if he gets out of hand at the company football game and tackles him out of bounds.

The concept of recognition involves the ability of a power structure to find a balance within an organizational context where the organization's general objective and specific tasks are sufficiently clear.

The democratic model that Hegel refers to with his example of the master and the slave, here seen in a very underdeveloped form, also presupposes that the State can be the context in which basic differences of power, knowledge and property can be brought into a situated balance.

It is hardly necessary to emphasize that it is a leader's task to be able to focus the organizational context in which opposing interests are brought into balance. He must actually be able to evoke the image of the joint effort or of the common cause that at once soothes tempers and brings harmony to the organization.

Hegel's thoughts are further developed in the phenomenological theory of inter-subjectivity, which is associated with J.-P. Sartre. His philosophical scoop was to analyse the experience of the other through the gaze. The gaze is the fundamental way in which we simultaneously accept that the other person is as real as we are *and* we make him an object precisely through the gaze that makes him real for us. In a very real sense, it determines our "regard" for the other. The English have an expression that captures this objectification of the other metaphorically: "looking babies". It means that we see ourselves in the other person's pupil and iris as if it were a little mirror. That is, we don't reveal to the other that we see that he sees us.

In sum, then, whether the other is a mystery by virtue of his power or his powerlessness, what is important is to draw him into the company's community where we can come to count on him. In single stroke, recognition establishes a common obligation, which may not depend on an absolute consensus, but nonetheless takes a broad view of whatever differences of opinion there may be. And as we know from the cultivation of the implicit and the tacit, it is the gaze, with the possible exception of the touch that provides the strongest expression of a heartfelt and obligated "Yes!"

The desire for the other can also be entangled in the game of power. We know this from all of the wonderful phenomena that occurs between the sexes. Seduction has its particular and peculiar role to play in processes of mutual recognition and consent. From here we can quite clearly see how complicated it is to understand the substantiality of and the motives behind consent in other areas of life. In other words, we become particularly aware of the *strategic* dimensions of recognition when we consider the reality of the erotic, perhaps because the tragic and the comic are so closely knit here.

But naturally, in the world of work strategic recognition also exists – as it does between colleagues and vertically within the hierarchies. Throughout the organization there is a serious interest in understanding who the other is.

Recognition, which is so indispensable to a new leader, can easily be given to him by the few, yet be denied to him by the informal fellowships or "clubs" that are found within the organization. He can feel that the only thing they are waiting for is a sign of his weakness. In this sense the game of recognition is cruel, from kindergarten to the retirement home.

It is therefore extremely important that the leader is able to interrupt the game of recognition.

He does this by being generous and meaning it. And he does this by having the objectivity that is required to give presence to the necessity of all of the organization's parts as well as by having a clear sense of the merits of these parts in the organization's history.

Generosity and related emotions, such as what Aristotle called 'magnanimity' (megalopsychia), claiming that the magnanimous person should display his magnanimity to his subordinates but not to his superiors, can only compensate for recognition where there's a reason for it. Otherwise the leader is interpreted as condescending or careless. When employees display such feelings toward the boss, it can easily be interpreted as opportunism or sucking up. Conversely, ironic, closed or harsh employees are a (well-known) nightmare for the inexperienced leader.

Integrity is, generally speaking, more powerful than generosity. Integrity holds a philosophical position in Aristotle's ethics and in the legal tradition of the West. Aristotle called the type of integrity that expresses a moderate magnanimity or a down-to-earth generosity "epieikeia". In Latin it is translated as "aequitas" and as "equity" in English. In Roman law it came to function as an important concept: the demand that the judge takes into consideration the situation and condition of the accused when he judges him. In Danish, originating from German, this concept is known as "billighed", which also evokes "affordability". We'll encounter this again during the discussion of the virtues of the leader.

Integrity, like generosity, borders on the game of recognition because it is ready to give more than it takes. One can then object that it is also a strategy. Maybe it is, but it works when it is used correctly, even though it can be painful sometimes.

Through integrity and generosity the other's right to maintain his mystery is preserved. These attitudes uphold freedom within organizations.

Today, many businesses increasingly muscle their way into the personal space of the individual. They want to be a part of his innermost thoughts because they want to exploit his dreams and his fantasies in order to get him to work harder, more passionately, and more ambitiously. To do this is to exploit recognition strategically, and sooner or later it will be found out and will have repercussions. It is the shadow side of the opportunities leaders have to deploy genuine feelings for strategic ends, where we may ultimately lose the employee's trust. It is then that the employees demand the right simply to punch in and punch out.

With this in mind we can also emphasize how important it is not to use consensus too strategically.

It is always arguable whether it is the seduced person who knows too little of what her 'Yes!' implies, or whether it is the seducer who imagines himself to be more than he is. But it is really not debatable that consensus within organizations ought to depend on a sufficient level of knowledge, information and openness, along with a right to various types of vetoing, if it is not to be considered utterly strategic.

It is a luxury to insist on people's adherence to a set of values if content, and thus consequences, haven't been carefully checked by all interested parties. When we start "outsourcing" the recognition of persons or actual communities, construing it simply as a matter of consenting to values, then we are dealing with second hand recognition, and this can be costly for the company in the long run. Immanuel Kant's wry comment from his last great book, *The Critique of Judgment*, is worth noting. Here, he points out that the common belief that enthusiasm results in better execution of one's tasks is an illusion. What the enthusiast really does is to deposit his freedom elsewhere.

2. The Other's reality is built into the forms of our communication

The stoics conceived of language as what sets people apart from all other living creatures. Today, we would call it "communication".

As speaking or writing beings, we often don't get to think first. It rushes out of us. It is because the words are so wrapped up in thoughts and feelings that some have claimed that we are word-machines. Even when we stop to think, we "talk to ourselves".

But we can only be like this because all of us are this way at the same time—though at times with varying intensity. The chess machine that beat Napoleon turned out to have a midget inside of it. This did not undermine our respect for the midget, only the credibility of the term 'chess machine'. We will not settle for a notion of "aliens" who master the language. Either we're computers, one and all, or else we're not.

Language can constitute a world as primordial as that of experience and the body, as the French philosopher Maurice Merleau-Ponty proposed. Thus, language should not be perceived as an "expression" of something else. When you speak, you do not communicate the content of some inner language of thought or imagery. Speech comes first. Whatever our thoughts may have in mind, language beats us to it.

When I understand another, I neither translate his speech nor his gestures into a unit of meaning that appears in my mind as something different from what he is saying. Thus, "meaning is in the word and in the comportment," as Merleau-Ponty says. To speak is therefore already to anticipate another's meaning, which can at most comprise a repetition or reiteration, an appropriated mime, but not a translation. Because in the structure of language, in speech itself, conversation is built-in, and thus the other is presupposed as the alter ego (the "other self").

To understand a threatening gesture I do not recall my own feelings of being threatened in the past as the basis of an interpretation of the threatening gesture. The threatening gesture *is* the threat.

My body is the instrument that spontaneously makes speech and gesture meaningful, as though meaning could be out in the world, somewhere between him and me.

But Merleau-Ponty emphasizes that the word constitutes the possibility of "blind recognition", which makes sensation real and precedes any intellectual preparation of meaning. This can be seen in the process of socialization, as it has been described by the Swiss psychologist and philosopher Jean Piaget:

The child only comes to experience an object as familiar when it is named. The name is part and parcel of the object, just like its color and its form.

"The word lives in the thing," said Merleau-Ponty.

For Merleau-Ponty, then, speech becomes the function through which the relationship of language to the world and consciousness stands out in its essence. For the child as well as the adult, language is what is most primordial and genuine about speech. But speech is nevertheless "instituted". We only have words if others give meaning to us. "Language takes care of itself," because meaning is supplied through a historical community. We learn language from others, and language in this sense always belongs to the others; we must use words that others can understand if we wish to be understood. Language originates with others. The linguistic expressions that express my individuality are always those of others.

Emmanuel Lévinas articulated this way of thinking in the book *Totality and Infinity,* written in the middle of the 20th Century. In this work he puts the student-teacher relationship in the center of sense-making.

The Virtue of Leadership

> *It is the transitivity of education and not the interiority of experience that makes being manifest. Truth is found in society. The moral relationship to the teacher who judges me, who supports the freedom I have to ally myself with the truth. Language arises by this means.*[6]

We meet this strong teacher in the business community perhaps most distinctly as the leader who is at the top of his career. In a moderate form we also encounter him as a "mentor" but not as the coach because the function of the coach is determined by a role, not a function that emerges from particular capacities (even though it demands knowledge and talent of particular kinds). It is crucial here to keep in mind that the teacher's identity is full of oppositions and tensions, even when it is separated from the person and is "merely" perceived as "the holy scripture" of the management guru's "ten commandments". The use of indoctrination, silver bullets and manipulative quick fixes as the foundation of quasi-totalitarian organizational cultures is the shadow side of the image of "the good teacher".

Both Merleau-Ponty's and Lévinas' ideas about the dominating role of language for experience and recognition accord with the Austrian philosopher Ludwig Wittgenstein who, in his later works, introduced the concept "language game". This concept has come to express the idea that we are prisoners of a given set of conditions for the expression of meaning, conditions that we can never fully command. These conditions can be shifted slowly throughout history along with the changes in what Wittgenstein called our "forms of life". The concept "form of life", which originates from phenomenological philosophy, has become, together with the concept "language game", one of this ultramodern philosopher's most central concepts. Both express the fact that meaning emerges in our practices, and that we are denied any hope of rising above this practice, i.e., any hope of discussing it in a "meta language", i.e., a language which isn't itself a part of this practice. But *language game* shouldn't be understood in a narrow sense of "codes". That idea has been developed by Basil Bernstein in the book *Class, Codes and Control*, according to which the classes have their particular "language". Nor is a language game simply a "culture", as Schein has suggested with the concept "corporate culture". We can speak of organizations having certain particular "codes", but we can't

---

[6] *Totality and Infinity* by Emmanuel Lévinas p. 95

call them particular language games. A language game refers to *regional ontologies*, i.e., to very comprehensive sides of existence. We have, perhaps, one language game for the beautiful and one for the good, and in Western European culture perhaps also one for the relationship between body and soul. But it could hardly be said that Denmark has a particular language game, much less that the Danish shipping magnate Mærsk Mc-Kinney Møller should have one. In these contexts we have idioms, dialects and codes.

These thoughts that have been presented to us are of great importance in understanding the function of dialogue in the organization and also in understanding the role that a language internal to the organization can play.

The scope of this language isn't wide, but there are commonplaces in communication that function as hidden imperative to feel, to think and to believe in a specific way. The commonplace way that language is fused with body and mind is the prerequisite for successful communication. But there is also a danger.

In this sense, we owe it to the other to help him to extricate himself from language and appear before us; just as we owe it to ourselves to cast off the disguises that language implicates us in. Ease of communication is more often a yoke than a gift.

It is the task of the leader to detach language from its commonplaces.

He is therefore at war with hot air, with allusions, with obvious arm-twisting, and with "that's how it's done around here", which is no longer followed by the provincial justification, "because that's how we've always done it", but by a much more dangerous presumption: "because it's efficient".

But you can't just create a distinctive, organizational "language" overnight; indeed, you can't create a language even given years. Local cultures allow only very few new games to be played with language because their members' use of language is constantly adjusted to the larger society, of which they're also members. The attempt to create new linguistic codes very easily winds up in the traps of rhetoric or indoctrination. In the first instance members are persuaded to believe that the banal concepts that they're persuaded to use have a particular meaning. In the other instance they're programmed to think in the way that they speak. But the leader can sabotage linguistic codes that lead to dead ends. Like the philosopher, he can question the most dangerous thing of all: the obvious, the glare of neon that has been frozen into words.

Also, this perspective, where the other is provided as a function of the use of speech and of its common dimensions point toward the need to understand a dialogue in the organization as something other and more than that which automatically confirms a prejudice. But because a person is embroiled in language, it appears with greater clarity how important it is to put a stop to illusions and consensus.

Consensus is indeed actually already anticipated in the way in which we associate words with each other and with things: as if we knew what they meant, and as if they always meant the same thing. Fundamentalism, of any observance derives its power over the mind from a monopoly on both power and authority in the interpretation of the written scriptures, an interpretation that appears so commonplace that it excludes anyone who might even suspect the possibility of another interpretation. Theocracies can also be found in private businesses and in public administration. Woe is he who violates the power of this silent brotherhood!

Leadership today is about daring to do the impossible. But the impossible differs from the outlandish in the sobriety of the words you use to describe the brave new world. What is impossible articulates a critical distance toward the concepts and images through which it draws attention to itself. It acknowledges a difficulty by pulling itself up by the hair. The outlandish ruthlessly exploits these concepts and thus exploits the content of its own message—regardless of whether or not it takes the receiver to be naïve.

Indeed, leadership today is very much about putting established buzzwords to the test.

It is comical, if almost tragic, to note that all Danish companies, for example, generally speaking have the same values. Getting out of this vicious circle can only be accomplished by the organization that is capable of making them real and thus incorporating them under the leadership that understands it, allowing all interested parties to play a part in the interpretation of the text. It isn't possible to replace these value-buzzwords because the result is would be an affected one, a new kind of chic that we already know from branding: "Responsibility first" and "Your child's future is our concern".

And if you want to insist on replacing them, a mad dash would ensue to be first to say the same thing in a new and clever way. But different companies have different responsibilities in society, even if their responsibilities toward their employees are more or less the same. They don't have the same stake holders, and their seriousness with regard to their intentions is best captured by being concrete. "Get the trains running on time!" Everybody knows what that means.

3. The event through which the Other comes into existence for me

What happens between people isn't exhausted in speech. Nobody can control the situation perfectly, regardless of how well spoken he may be, and nobody can control the other or himself. It is therefore clear that what is called dialogical philosophy concerns the conditions of conversation that lie beyond what is said. Dialogue is about the encounter, and the encounter is willy-nilly an event. Modern philosophy of dialogue thus differentiates itself from the classical Greek "dialectic" because events are essentially autonomous. It is by no means certain that the given situation can be brought to its conclusion, let alone its climax.

The climax is a figure that lurks in every consensus and in every dialogue—but not necessarily in recognition because recognition can be maintained in a tension.

If we say that a *situation* is a condition that can be approached strategically by accounting for its most important parameters, then an *event* is something that happens to us that we can't approach instrumentally. In this sense a meeting resembles an event, even if the management has set it up. This is the realm of the unpredictable.

Philosophers have attempted to express this conceptually by asserting that the subject of a dialogical encounter is neither of its interlocutors but, on the contrary, the encounter itself. There is an inertial power at work in the meeting itself that extends well beyond what its interlocutors have to offer, and therefore well beyond the reach of an agenda.

People who are occupied with dialogue in practice, such as politicians, leaders, negotiators, therapists, and teachers have a tendency to notice an independent realm between the speakers only when the conversation takes an unexpected turn and draws in something new. But during an ordinary business meeting we are generally ill-disposed to see this third space, this interstice, which the German-Jewish philosopher Martin Buber, writing at the beginning of the previous century, described as a natural boundary.

But the situation in which you meet another or several people precisely reflects a limitation in the space of possibility that is available for experiencing the other in new ways. Its built-in functionality, which is so pronounced in most situations in the business world, can anticipate what is different; it can project, overlap or exclude the sense of something new, deadening our sensitivity for the contours of a new and common "possible world".

The meeting as an "interstice", a "place between", of course, can all too often erect a wall between people. But it always contains a potential common ground, sometimes available simply by the gentle turning of a well-known phrase, a "commonplace" remark that opens a space of free expression. The good leader understands the importance of fostering and maintaining this potential. Nothing could be further from this understanding than the act of intimidation.

A wall exists because the interlocutors try with all their might to get the meeting to go their way, to "promote their agenda". And thus, through this strategic attitude, they have already imposed severe restrictions on the opportunities available for progress towards that which is not yet in hand, indeed, they have cut themselves off from a way to leverage the potential implicit precisely in its not yet being upon us. It is a free space, or a space that requires freedom in order to exist, because the leader must by no means undermine the employees' initiative and need to take responsibility.

There is much, then, to suggest that the "theory" of the other that we need today will have to construe the meeting in terms of the encounter, which is to say, as an event that unfolds in the interstices between speakers and which is capable transforming the whole situation from the inside. Our multicultural societies, combined with the prevalence of interdisciplinary practices, and our subjection to a future that must be approached despite our inability to anticipate it by strategic means, force us to be prepared to meet people, not nakedly, or "face to face", but rather as speakers of a language that is formed by contexts, themselves shaped the shifting of uncertain and often doubtful agendas.

The event does not belong to anyone. It happens, and it happens right over the heads of the planners of contemporary mega-happenings, the so-called "events" of event management. It turns the orchestrated demonstration of power inside out, and it pushes strategies down the inexorably slippery slope that is marked by the question, "What are we doing this *for*?" which, in turn, is concealed in the sarcasm of the employee who dares to ask, "Are we having fun yet?" when it is obviously already too late.

Experiencing the Other

The skilful leader should understand that there are limits to what you can prepare yourself for. He already knows that there are limits to what you can plan.

But our awareness of this particular species of impotence should not occasion our indignation; on the contrary, this awareness, when it is cultivated in its pure form, simply expresses a sense of the opportunities contained in all that hasn't yet happened.

We should construe the meeting as a "no man's land". By virtue of its fertile neutrality, it contains seeds and traces of light that lead us out beyond the horizon of the expected. The horizon of the expected itself is always strategic. It is drawn by our ulterior motives and our more pretentious sentiments.

The opportunities available to you to teach yourself about the insurmountable chasm that runs between the situation and the event are everywhere present in your organization. The trick is to prepare yourself for a surprise that you have yourself arranged (not only for the others but also for yourself), especially in the space that you set aside for coaching. If you can disdain to decide in advance that your employees are to toe the line, then something good can happen.

That is why coaching is so interesting: not because we have to take to heart glad tidings of our therapeutic society in our organizations, but because coaching, as an example of dialogical consciousness, can give us ideas toward entirely new forms of leadership. Coaching can teach us precisely to respect the encounter implicit in every meeting and thus make us ready for events.

Or, putting it differently, if our leaders take their meetings and dialogues seriously the event will arrive all by itself.

Chapter 9

The Organizational Perspective

I have now described the demands that can be made of the leader, and which pertain to human understanding. These demands also open a space of opportunity that allows for new attitudes toward life and work, new ways of understanding and treating others. Indeed, in the final analysis, they may open a space of freedom. The leader has here been construed as though his role in the organization could be described solely from his own perspective. We have, in other words, looked at other people, the community (and, therefore, the organization in general) in the light of the leader's task of stepping into character.

But the leader, like any other human being, is not just a finished product of his social contexts; these also continually foster and shape him, imbuing him with his reality.

Although leaders often arrive as strangers to existing organizations, they have both a right and a duty to stand apart from the organization. So, for better or for worse, a leader is in an important sense dependent on the character of the very social relations that it is his job to establish and to maintain, and which he can, if he is up to it, make render ever more intense in their transformation.

It is entirely too superficial and strategic to describe the leader's relationship with his employees as "communication". There are far more fundamental connections at work. "Communication" is a technical term, which refers to the economical and efficient management of messages, construing these as knowledge resources that can be distributed through more or less lucrative exchanges. Not incidentally, it considers messages in terms of the content they convey, e.g., by establishing measures for the quantity of signs that have been transferred. A company can, of course, be conceived of in this way because the spectrum of solicitations can be delineated strategically, even if they can't be controlled. But the strategic approach comes up short when the relation that must be established to the employees is taken into consideration. Moreover, the public sphere has become generally more reflective and, in a sense, more intelligent. After all, it now has rather extensive experience with what are often very sophisticated attempts at image management. Here it is all about human relationships that may well call for a strategic perspective in some isolated, situational contexts, but which generally require another approach.

All organizations consist of a complicated interplay of formal and informal communities, of systemic and organic wholes, and it is the greatest task of the leader to understand the difference between them and be able to detect the axes of power and possibility that occupy the centre of the informal operative communities. These are really the resources of the company because they contain the real and virtual *cooperative capacities* that are the secret of the innovative and dedicated employee behaviour that is likely to bring results. Strategic overtures can destroy the full exploitation of this reservoir of innovative and obligating opportunities. This insight does not, of course, make strategy in organisation superfluous; it only installs it in a context that is better suited to the times in which we live.

A good example of this can be seen in the way the leader makes his choice of heir known to the organization. Such signals can be sent in many ways. They can consist in the simple deferral of the decision in order to force "political" tensions within the organization to light. It can consist in leaving it up to the employees themselves. Or it can consist in a clear and unambiguous announcement of one's priorities as to policy and person[7]. The leader's generosity can show itself here because it takes a lot of personal integrity to have the courage to choose an heir who can, will and dares to do his own thing. The history of states and companies is absolutely rife with examples of choices of heirs whose personal and moral weakness when compared with "the grand old man" has had fatal consequences for the institution he has built.

The community is about the ways in which *comprehensive wholes* exist in organizations. But the concept of a "whole" is just as complicated as it is overused.

Any organization an be construed as a system, that is, as a whole that can be taken to be so tangible that it can be made the object of analyses for the purpose of delineating its structure, form, causal relationships, functional relationships and mechanisms generally. A system will often be construed as something that can be approached intellectually through the image of a machine, while wholes are normally understood to be organic entities, where it is precisely the *whole* that is

---

[7] Max De Pree emphasizes the importance of the leader's choice of heir at an early stage. In my opinion, De Pree's books about leadership constitute some of the best American popular literature that has ever been written on the topic. See his *Leadership as an Art* and *Leadership Jazz* from 1989 and 1992 respectively.

greater than the parts. Where the machine only becomes greater than the sum of its parts when it is running, the organic is in itself something that plies the parts into a whole that can in some sense be said to exist "prior to" it.

But to speak of a "system" often presupposes one or more privileged points in the organization from which to view it; there must be a sort of objective authority that can take up a position outside the system itself. This is problematic when seen from the point of view of a theory of knowledge or a theory of science because we are then simply granted a third "language" in which to describe our dialogues and this, of course, is no guarantee of truth. We can compound the difficulty by adding that a whole, when seen from the perspective of a system, is often construed as being virtually closed, which there is no reason to think an organization is today.

The concept of a whole is so fragile today because companies are open to the world through the planned and spontaneous formation of networks, but also because companies are increasingly becoming just another public space situated in a national and global public sphere. This means that a company is always itself a part of a more comprehensive whole that has the power to shape it. We must therefore be very careful when we use concepts like "whole", "system" and "community" without first having very precisely defined our context and, therefore, the logic of our assertions' content and extension.

There are many problems associated with the concept of "whole" itself, even if it is introduced in the company of fine grained distinctions and with great conscientiousness. We can shed light on these problems as they arise in connection with the application of Søren Kierkegaard's thought, which has become the most plausible basis for an understanding of the perspective of existential philosophy on organizations. This perspective is becoming increasingly relevant the more we focus on leadership as the personal development of the leader himself and of his employees. Even if it is wholly plausible to apply Kierkegaard's "steps" from *Either-Or*, which are also known under the title of another of his books, namely, *Stages on Life's Way*, and thus distinguish between the "aesthetic", the "ethical" and the "religious" states or stages available within organizations and in people, this must be done with great many caveats, which are not confined to the difficulties of applying the "religious" stage to business units and economic agents.

Even a cursory examination of the implications of Kierkegaard's ideas about the relation of the individual to the society reveals that he invokes only personal relations, that is, only relations between concrete individuals, and only situations in which the individual can represent himself. This individual can never act on behalf of a common weal, nor can he act by virtue of a formal or authoritative community. To put the point as sharply as possible, there is a clear dilemma between Kierkegaard's starting point in the individual and all the generalized entities that our use of the concept of "whole" encompasses when it is applied in a business context.

This dilemma can not be disposed of simply by pointing out that all wholes are conceptual constructs because wholes operate as realities in the lives of individuals. Wholes exist as so-called intentional objects. I relate to the "nation", the "region", the "continent", the "alliance" and the "team". We own stocks in "IBM" and "Microsoft". We are incensed by "the tabloids" and concerned about "Islam". We identify leaders with their organizations even if we are legally bound to go after individuals when we want to indict the actions that are carried out under the banners of major corporations.

There can hardly be any doubt that our common sense presumes that wholes can be more than the sum of their parts. That, in fact, is a positive presupposition for imagining the development of organisations into functional "organisms". And the leader *must*, of course, confront his company as a whole if he is to embrace its organization and maintain its distinction from the environment. Otherwise he will become so nearsighted that all he sees are divisions and departments. This is fatal. Command of the situation demands working with wholes; there is no way around this.

Kierkegaard used his intellect passionately to show that the whole—whether it be the state, the church or what the German philosopher Hegel called "the world spirit", which has a monopoly on the truth because it so "clever" that it can incorporate all our objections against it, yes, even the unintended ones, and assimilate them in its grand logic of ends—always undermines the individual's capacity to take responsibility for himself. To cite an overarching "cause" is to abdicate one's sovereignty and thereby one's claim to legitimacy in the name of the whole. But the act of referring to an idea need not have these disempowering consequences, and this is the hidden paradox in Kierkegaard's philosophy: causes and ideas are not the same thing. We can learn a great deal from this because ideas can denote ideals and norms, opportunities to think, feel and live out an attitude toward life, and yet without finally having to hoard it for oneself. "Causes", meanwhile, and increasingly also "values", are to a much greater extent introduced through power and in a context that ties them to institutional and doctrinaire demands that conceal strategic criteria of success.

Let us turn this around and ask whether Kierkegaard does not really also deploy a concept of community—a community that does not at the same time betray the position of the individual in a historical process.

One thing is certain. Even if the game of chance and the designs of power in the great theatre of history can only be understood if one has the biographer's eye for the importance of the individual ("dictator" is not just a role that anyone could have played), they cannot be fully comprehended and by that means approached pragmatically, that is, as a basis for liberating action in the future, unless one admits that wholes have a decisive influence. This insight also pertains to business: we cannot do justice to the individual leader and innovator if we do not understand the context of wholes that comprises the conditions of his actions and which in their capacity as companies and institutions become the result of his actions. We must have an eye for agents and structures, as we said in the 1980s; but we must also have an eye for self-creation ("autopoiesis") and systems, for spontaneous sense-making, for the positive role of reasonable critiques and for the role that automatic "discursive machines" (concepts and arguments in relation to given problems, which seems to be *the* obvious procedure) play in the creation of the organization's inner space.

Philosophy has not progressed one-two-three from the individual (monologue) to the relationship between two persons (dialogue) through the relationship between three people (trialogue) and from there on to the whole or the mass. Rather, in classical Greek philosophy and on to age of romanticism, the individual has been confronted with the state (society), but there has been little interest in the way that two people relate to each other in an abstract sense. One notable exception here is the "neighbour" of Christianity. Two other epochal and liberating exceptions are constituted by Plato's focus on the "majeutic dialectic", that is, on way Socrates served as a "midwife" in the birth of his student's ideas, which is to say, the liberating conversation, and Aristotle's theory of friendship from the *Nichomachean Ethics*. This new focus on the concreteness of the relationship between two people is emphasised by Hegel in the beginning of the 1800s. Before that, the relationship to the other was characterised only in terms of a very abstract image of one's "neighbour" without appealing to any specific social identity. One was more interested in the relation between cosmos and chaos as the content of the totality that individuals must relate to, depart from and be swallowed up in. And they were of course interested in the relationship of the individual to the law, to *nomos*. *Power* always constitutes the point of view from which the individual and the whole are comprehended. It would take parliaments, peasant revolts, enlightenment values and utopian socialism, that is, substantial and institutional guarantees of the rights of the individual, before the relationship between two people could be construed abstractly beyond the images of power. The German philosopher Hegel, whom we've already discussed, is the decisive piece in beginning to put this enormous puzzle together. It came to form a picture of the positions of power that motivated the task of changing them: it became possible to make demands of it and to assign tasks to it, all of which were related to the fostering of legitimacy. But the basis of all legitimacy, like the basis of the dialectic of recognition, is *freedom*. Consent for the system is meaningless if it is not based on personal autonomy.

The Christian concept of one's "neighbour" emerges from a sense of how destructive power can be but its institutional development, its theology, does not include a critique of power as the right of mastery through authority, position or property. The Christian Church has only in the past decade really chosen to distinguish between an intimate power's negative effects and the destructive human consequences of structural power, including that of the capitalist system. An example, here, is the Catholic Church's opposition to totalitarian systems of government in South America. Christianity affirmed the right to criticize and tied faith to the common good. It did this with the sanction of Martin Luther, who supported the brutal suppression of the peasant uprisings at the end of the Thirty Year War. It did not, however, develop a systematic analytical platform that sets itself the goal of comprehending the conditions of and opportunities for the remission of power. The reality in which power is rescinded is deferred until the millennium and the return of Christ or left to writers and proselytizers. Christian movements that had the goal of social equality and the rejection of all exercises of power were often suppressed by the state churches or isolated as sects (the Quakers, for example). In Christianity, each individual must take responsibility for what he does to his neighbour, find a way to make up for the transgressions that follow from his own exercises of power. But he is not committed to abdicating his power; he is bound only to keep himself from exploiting it in illegitimate ways (which, of course, is much more than simply following customary practice.)

The Organizational Perspective

Kierkegaard, however, approaches this problem very differently. While we have to be careful, we can say that Kierkegaard's epochal contribution to Christianity was to construe it in the light of a conception of personal freedom. For him, freedom was bottomless. There is never any guarantee that a human being has done *enough*. The spirit, as the Apostle Paul also noted, remains above the law. It serves as the passion of faith—and passion, in contrast to desire or lust, is characterised by not relying on built in criteria for it own satisfaction.

Hegel is the great contrast to Kierkegaard because he begins to think of power in terms of a necessary stage in the progress towards making its own remission a theme for reflection. Power carries its own sublimation within itself because it presupposes its recognition by at least one other person. Recognition therefore installs freedom in the logic of power itself. Recognition is complicit. It is reciprocal by nature. If one wants to be recognized as a master then one must recognize the slave that is the real basis of one's power. You are only free if you realize that you owe your freedom to the freedom of another, and vice versa. In a miniature world populated by only one human being and a thousand robots, the human being would never really be able to be recognized for his power, not to mention his freedom, but only for his technical skill. Recognition demands flesh and eyes. As Sartre noted, its central medium of communication is the gaze. Recognition presupposes the freedom of those who would restrain and bind, precisely by virtue of this gesture of recognition. The respect that is shown in the potential "recognizer" is and remains strategic. Freedom is in this context unfree.

Hegel's brilliant analysis of recognition in the *Phenomenology of the Spirit* from 1807 shows us that power is in principle maintained at an interpersonal level, i.e., one-on-one. That is why its cruelty is also directed at the individual. Dictators have always had a very keen sense of the individuals that can confirm their power, and of those who cannot. In totalitarian ages, a one-to-one balance between these two groups of people has been approximated. But is has never been fully accomplished. Regimes have found it necessary to garner support by base forms of recognition that made sophisticated networks of terror possible at second hand and therefore produced cannon fodder.

But now that the age of giant regimes of terror seems to be passing and terror on the factory floor is no longer available to those who would improve productivity—and least not in Western industrial societies—the leader is confronted with the facts of recognition.

For now, we can construe the organization as a series of processes through which recognition is communicated at different levels.

In the spirit of Kierkegaard it is immediately incumbent on us to distinguish between genuine and false recognition, and therefore between genuine and false behaviour, between processes and structures in the communication of recognition.

What Kierkegaard does, and which makes his philosophy superior to Hegel's functional universe of the system, is to conceive of a freedom that can be realized in practice without having to take it from another.

This peculiar form of freedom is expressed through Christ. For the recognition of Christ does not occur through an exchange of power characterized by functional reciprocality, but through powerlessness, that is, through *faith*[8].

One abdicates one's power through faith, and thereby one's freedom. You put your freedom in someone else's hands by demonstrating trust and confidence or unconditional loyalty. Most people will of course see this where something is expected in return. But what you get back is not access to a role that grants anything like a divine right.

Our relationship with the leader must of course not be understood in this image. An organization is not a church, and the leader is not a substitute for God. But it is worth seeing that there exists an antidynamic of recognition that can relate itself to the interplay of power and freedom through a *"no"*.

In other words, the experience of the other as a human being on equal footing with oneself can also be seen through the image of trust, just as the Danish philosopher K. E. Løgstrup proposed in his book *The Ethical Challenge*, using the argument that it mirrors the child's relationship with the world. There are relationships to people, and even organizations, where the point of departure is not suspicion, but rather trust. Where this is the case, the shame that befalls one who abuses it is correspondingly greater.

We can also put it as follows. The genuine leader must strive to meet people in such a way that they do not need to imagine that the basic mechanism in human relations is necessarily power.

If we examine the reality of work today in practical and concrete terms, we can say that unless we have eye for the fact that classical forms of formalized recognition no longer have any power to speak of,

---

[8] "Belief" is called "pistis" in Greek. "Pistis" also means "confidence", "trust" and "loyalty".

we simply can't understand the hypermodern organization, with its well educated employees and its leaders who transmit humanistic policy statements to support the administration of their power. Pay raises, stock options, the stereo in the company car, pleasurable business trips and so forth are no longer considered fully valid expressions of recognition. There are, of course, a lot of reasons for this, but it is owed first and foremost to an unspoken consensus that the basis of the organization is interpersonal relations between leader and employee and that this relationship, moreover, is to be understood as a variant of the common human relationship between two people.

We can also say that recognition is only granted on a background of legitimacy.

Legitimacy is about the ability to justify one's actions through an idea. An idea does not have to be identical with a cause, because a cause is tied to special interests no matter how "good" it is. Ideas are not. They can be cultivated by anyone at any time.

Legitimacy, further, means that recognition cannot be arbitrary, that is, not primarily tied to specific connections between the leader and the employee (e.g., owing to family ties or shared membership is one or another club, or because the leader does not want to admit that he has hired the wrong person for the job, or employed the wrong head hunter, etc.). Recognition must be objective, that is, it must be founded on the submission of both the sender and the receiver to an articulated set of criteria or valuable social action. At the same time, the one who receives recognition must really have deserved it; that is, recognition must not be partisan, arbitrary or contrived. The weight of recognition is directly proportional with the moral integrity of the one who gives it. And the effect of recognition is directly proportional with the extent to which the one who receives it feels that there are good reasons for it. The administration of recognition therefore demands moderation, even frugality. Just as orders lose their value in proportion to their dispersion, so too does recognition. Recognition, finally, must be an expression of the fact that he who receives it is able to balance a regard for himself with regard for the community. Giving egoists and narcissists the recognition they want only works in some situations and never in the long run.

We can here see that as soon as we start talking about recognition, we also start talking about collective entities like ideas, ideals and criteria, and about wholes like "community". It is impossible to entertain a sound opinion about the individual in an organisational context if one does not master this vocabulary.

If we can therefore conclude that recognition can only be given and received on a presumption of authority then this implies also a presumption of independence. But neither of these can be understood as the result of a subjective application of effort. They are anchored into a context. This means that authority must be garnered from a set of ideas that are sanctioned by the living community. Authority cannot stand on its own because it would then become a merely "psychological" phenomenon. It must proceed from a set of common values.

Independence cannot mean that one "creates oneself" at the expense of others. The authority that stems from critique can only be legitimate if it is based on a sense of responsibility for a community.

Recognition and authority thus stem from a community. But how are we to think of this community in a Kierkegaardian context?

Chapter 10

The Intangible Community

If we distinguish between, on the one hand, formally cohesive communities like nation-states, directorates and traditional firms and, on the other hand, spontaneous, quite informal communities, even wholly devoid of a unifying theme, such as those that can arise between tourists on a charter tour, then we will discover that most organizations occupy a place somewhere in between, for the sole reason that they are forced to transform themselves in a rhythm that is determined by their surroundings. Communities of the first kind are wholes that are in the main held together by a single mechanism: the law.

The law is *the* exceptional, principled expression of the existence of the whole and the surest sign of stability, a stability that need not be presupposed when we note, both empirically and historically, that the whole really has survived. This last is fraught with difficulties, however, at least when seen from a logical and analytical point of view, for what does it mean to say that an organization is "the same" when the majority of its employees and leaders are gone, when the product has changed, and when the offices have been moved to a new location, so that only the name remains? In a context beyond the nation-state, the law is a complicated concept because it at one and the same time refers to formal and informal organizational procedures. In that sense, one can easily seize upon the distinction between *the letter of the law* and *the spirit of the law*, which has been developed by the Gospels, by the Apostle Paul and by Plato (most famously in his "second letter" and of course in the discussion we find in his later dialogue *The Laws*).

For it is obvious that to the extent that an organization is calculated to deal with changing contexts so too must the spirit of the law, the *ethos* of the organization, predominate over its letter. An organization that is undergoing expansion, change or even transformation must, when seen from a functionalistic perspective, be organizations that invoke their laws with a mixture of insight, circumspection and sense of the situation.

Nothing in history is a more apt display of this than Paul's letters. Here the overcoming of ethnic and religious egoism demands a revolt against the law and the prophets. The letter of the law must be replaced with faith, hope and love. These three basic concepts of the Apostle Paul are in any case the medicine that on a greater and a lesser scale have always been taken to combat the fever of legalism: faith as an image of the core of a new community, love as a way into it and hope as a vision of its progress from utopia to reality.

A functional account—which we *must* provide now and then in a business context—therefore displays the hypermodern organization as one that must partly replace the law with passion, that is, with the empathetic sense of its spirit and therefore with an understanding of the context in which it arose and the aims it served.

Now, it just so happens that this process is the recurring characteristic of Kierkegaard's works.

If we read Kierkegaard empathetically then we will see that he too refers to a community and precisely to community beyond the law. This is the community is that is forever being created by those who believe.

This community's formal sides are the "kerygma", the "word", the message, i.e. the reception of the holy scripture by the individual each and every moment in a way against the "temptation" ("peirasmón" as it occurs in the Lord's Prayer), which consists in not being able to believe. This scripture remains central, and its power is what keep fundamentalism at bay. This has not been accomplished by developments within the institutional framework for its interpretation, dissemination and enforcement; that is, it has not been accomplished by the churches.

The image of this moment, in which all human beings have the opportunity to confirm their sense of belonging to a living community is "kenosis"; "das Knechtwerdens Gottes", as Luther said; "God in time", as Kierkegaard put it; the inconceivable: the unity of the finite and the infinite, the eternal and the temporal. It is the paradox of the world he inhabited that God rescinds the "guile of infinity", which is what he calls death in his *Concluding Unscientific Postscript*. Or Jesus brings infinity close to us and categorically denies God's apparent anger with the world through his sacrifice on the cross.

But what does this have to do with the modern company or the public institution?

Quite a bit!

For this word, this message, is Kierkegaard's point of entry to not just the everyday creativity of the community, but to the preceding creation of the community itself. This happens by the affirmation of one's personal convictions, that is, one's "faith", which fills the New

Testament through the Greek word "pistis". But "pistis" also means "truth between people" in Greek philosophy, which is where the word comes from—it is the concept of "mutual loyalty".

With faith in God, our trust in others is enrolled in the same movement because the possibility that lets one appear before God also lets anyone else do so. Faith is the life of the idea in the soul of man. It is always superior to any "cause", which is merely its institutional translation as a programme.

We are here given a very relevant image of communities as something greater than formally sanctioned collaboration towards a contingent aim assisted by the means that are always and everywhere available and justified by an appeal to "enlightened self-interest". We are given an image of a spiritual community, which does not just *exist*, but must be continually created through a repetition that must itself conquer all automatism. But we are at the same time given a perspective that makes it possible to approach these promising and seductive communities in a critical manner, even if they stem from one's own hands, one's own mouth. We are given a community around a cause, which can always be corrected by the individual according to the way he interprets and appropriates its idea.

Kierkegaard's focus on the individual's responsibility for himself is thus not just commensurable with the idea of a community, but is presupposed by it, by Christianity remains a "movement" in a double sense, that is, both a spiritual community that one can join, and a dynamic organism, alive and kicking, which the individual cannot not only influence but the content and form of which he always has responsibility for because he is carried along with it.

One can think what one likes of Christianity, but in its various institutional and sectarian incarnations throughout the past two thousand years, and especially in the lead up to them, and within enclaves to these institutions, it expresses *the* only real non-aggressive manifestation of organic communities. That Catholicism is also one the largest, most successful attempts to create a uniform administrative context where the aim all too often has been used to justify the means is another matter that will not be addressed here.

In Christianity we can study the historical emergence of communities around an idea and we can study its institutional developments into apparatuses of power with a "cause" as its irrefutable content[9].

---

[9] It would be too comprehensive to include an analysis of the obvious complement to Christianity, which the transformation of political ideas and their ossification into ideologies through ideological and state apparatuses of power constitutes.

The exchange of forces between individual passion and commitment to a virtual community of believers, which is Kierkegaard's theme, can be transferred to the hypermodern organisation only if we take it with a grain of salt, perhaps a whole shaker. For it takes a good deal of acumen, tact and analytic discipline, along with no mean portion of critical sensitivity, to transfer religious experiences to profane, organizational contexts. We here meet the question of how a balance can be established between self-critical authority and devotion.

After all, it is natural to emphasise that the individual is not served by a community that lords over him, that guides him and directs him by way of feelings that are taken from the private sphere, feelings such as "love" (as Åkerstrøm Andersen and Born have recently shown in a book called *Love and Restructuring*). And it is important to note, on the other hand, that if stepping into character has been strategically imposed by the community as a proscribed act of "self-creation", then this does nothing to foster individual critical authority (as Åkerstrøm Andersen has shown in a recent book about the contractual exclusion of the individual from the community). Self-creation demands a free space, that is, spaces and processes in the organization that are free from the reach of strategy. This demands an emotional logistic directed at autonomy.

The institutional or organizational staging of passion is not just nauseating and inconvenient in the long run, it is also dysfunctional because it makes a convention of passion and strategically connects an empty concept of "self-creation" with administrative and bureaucratic interests.

I believe it is of paramount importance to follow Kierkegaard in search of those communities that, by virtue of their spontaneity and claim to continuous passionate maintenance, at the same time make it possible for the individual to preserve his integrity. It is here, as already mentioned, important always to be able to compare the *idea* to the *cause* because the idea is both a platform, from which the individual may at any time critically test the cause, and the dynamo that creates the communities that make causes possible.

These *intangible communities*—as I've chosen to call them—can be found in all organizations. They exist among the uneducated workers on the shop floor, among the members of the innovative team, in project groups, and even occasionally on the top floor. They can be found across the organizational hierarchies and all organizers dream of gaining access to them, for they are the treasure trove of the organization. They are also found across companies and generations. That is why we talk so often of "projects" and "networks", because we believe that these structures can impart a creative thrust that fosters intangible communities—a phenomenon that otherwise normally only arises on its own.

But almost more important than the intangible communities are the *utopian communities*. They express the idea that the organization can come finally to be about if the potential of all the employees is exploited to its fullest and if everyone is allowed to dream the dream that bad leadership is so good at suppressing. When communities become utopian, then the leader becomes a medium for the articulation of a power that he must himself have contributed to setting free.

It can hardly surprise anyone that muscles and ligaments in bodies of these intangible communities is *pistis*, belief in the idea, mutual trust and full support behind this "idea".

When I therefore in the parts to follow treat the classical components of systems—"wholes" such as "language", "culture" and "the spirit of organizations"—then I will precisely include them in the tension between individual authority, human development and the strengthening of discipline on the one side, and the spontaneous community on the other. It is natural to look at the organisation's "linguistic codes" in this perspective in order to be able to confront the hollow and functionally rhetorical use of language with that use that covers the body of the spontaneous community like a skin rather than trapping its breathing as in a diving suit

PART IV

THE NEW THEMES OF LEADERSHIP

Chapter 11

Of Narratives and Leaders

Today's leader must be able to deal with three themes: narration, presence and freedom. They all stem from the "logic" that characterizes developments in organizing in recent years.

Let us look at them in turn.

A. The Concept of Narration

The concept of *narration* comes from the Latin "narration", which gives us also "narrative" and "narrativity", which has passed from literary theory into ordinary language. It is complicated and difficult to deal with. This is owed to the fact that the concept of "narration" covers a space that extends from documentation at one end to pure make believe at the other, that is, from a registration of reality to that which does not pretend based in anything other than imagination. Between these poles, perhaps halfway, we find the "myth", a word which does not just denote a particular genre that can be traced back to almost prehistoric notion of a "legend", but is also used as an expression of the particular quality proper to good stories (narratives). For they contain a myth, which is to say, a universal structure, that brings the human condition to the fore in an exceptional way along with an awareness of the painfully composite nature of our minds. Plato long ago described the two-fold nature of myths. They are, on the one hand, they in which the experience of justice and goodness can be transmitted from generation to generation *and* the means by which this knowledge is trivialized or rendered superficial in its ties to the medium through which a myth moves: the mental image, the inner world of condensed sense experience. Images beckon us forward, and that is why myths can lead us astray from that which Plato believed was our genuine task as people: to perfect ourselves in relation to the divine meaning of the world and the moral and ethical demands made by the community and the other.

There are at least three ways that the narrative has become part of everyday living in what has been called "the society of experience".

- It has become the primary way that the major media address us. They do so in part through "the story", in part through

story-like "documents", in part through interviews that always refer to the interviewee's life and context, unless they are about matters of plain fact or involve politicians (whom we don't want to hear more about than we already know), and therefore to their personal biography.
- It is the basis of the content of the audio-visual media. Not only our entertainment, but even the dominant way of making news, must, virtually according to the "logic" of the media, take the form of reportage and therefore a nascent form of narrative. The international coverage of the war on Iraq showed this with all the clarity we could desire. News is increasingly centered on individuals, who come to stand for a particular theme that is addressed on screen. But they come easily to crush the human dimension in their eagerness to present emotionally authentic material.
- It has become a way in which the scientific institutions not only communicate their results but even produce them in their investigation of empirical phenomena. In that sense, the narrative is increasingly coming to replace arguments and schematic documentation. This can be justified as a reaction against the dominance of statistical methods in the reproduction of social reality and, therefore, as a reaction against a faith in our ability to generalize as well within the social sciences as is common practice in the domain of the natural sciences. And it can be justified, further, because a story can make tangible the fact that empirical reality must always be interpreted by a particular subject and thereby must be mirrored through a particular attitude to experience. But it is by no means obvious that our consciousness of this "subjectivity" or the inexorable prejudice of any perspective is communicated simply by the choice of narrative form. The opposite could also be the case.

In a forum where power has been reduced to a level below that which we find in democracies it is plausible to imagine that the best story would win out over less qualified contenders. This would require that all members of society had the same level and horizon of knowledge, experience, attitude and information. But stories often find themselves spinning their wheels today because they only tell us what we expect to hear. The mythical aspect of the great narratives, that which hits us squarely in the face and brings tears to our eyes, is always in a sense at war with time. They go their own way and they never finally undermine the brutal facts of power. They can sometimes even render historical conditions as though they were natural, and they can in that sense anticipate the Promethean revolt against the lot of man, which they invoke in the form of despair, indignation and empathy in relation to the characters of the story. They here show that it is all in vain. But narratives can also challenge us pursue historical justice and can therefore be censored and suppressed. It takes courage to be Emile Zola, whose novels defended the nascent socialist movements in the last third of the nineteenth century.

In the new millennium, when Nietzsche's old pronouncement "It is the right of the victors to name things", seems to be the motto of the gleeful storytellers, it is all too often successful people who *want* to tell their strategic stories. The stories that, by contrast, stem from just indignation are more difficult to tell unless they are about something that happens far, far away, and the social, economic and historical conditions of which we all agree are offensive.

The subterranean stories, the stories of the slaves and hussars, that were also in the beginning a part of the Christian narrative have either been safely lead in the port of the nation-state or have been given line item in one or another national budget. Not just our sense of justice, but also our indignation and despair, must today receive proper authentication.

We celebrate authenticity in order to sweep it under the carpet. If another John Howard Griffin emerges in the press, he will be so quickly put on a pedestal as an earnest genius and buried in journalistic prizes that we can comfortably forget the just indignation that was the basis of what he said.

B. The Basis of Narration

In their very nature, narratives stem from the mouth or hand of a single human being. We imagine that the individual must be their source. Later, after the first narrator's first narration has been heard its transmission is left to their repetition by many mouths, to be heard by many ears, and read by a thousand eyes. The written text offers a kind of exception to this repetition, which leaves the transformation of the story that the oral transmission of long stories cannot avoid to the reader, which is to say, to interpretation. The printer and bookbinder conserve the details of the story in a sense, because it repeats the exercise of the author without physically changing the story.

But the fact that the tale, the narration, the good story (in some corners of popularised management theory one generally supposes that poor narratives don't exist or that the good story will, in any case, always win out—but no one ever says what it is that constitutes the particular "goodness" of a good story) stems from one mouth and one hand leads us to believe that it can also be created. By analogy with craftsmanship and the conscious action, we imagine that stories can be fabricated. Nothing could be more mistaken. Stories that contain the power of myth doe not arise *overnight*. The come into being, they arise, they suddenly arrive and they surprise no one more that the one who we uncritically identify as their originator as if it was perfectly natural to do so.

Stories are emergency baptisms at sea, far more than they are made to order epigraphs and epitaphs. They are dodges rather than jabs into a world that is fat and well nourished with words, organizations eager to brand, actors demanding an image.

We are fooled into believing that we can glean the structural power of narratives as long as we, who analyse them, can indicate the traces of a "sculptural logic" that pleases by virtue of its balanced form.

Narratives are something altogether different. They are messages that hid themselves in the story that is told as figure in an optical illusion.

Narratives do not just hide the story they tell but also the storyteller. They leave the meaning of what is said to posterity. And if they are really good, like the fairy tales, myths and parables that we feel ourselves tied to in our thoughts and our experiences because they inhabit our recollections with such great naturalness, then they belong to everyone and to no one.

When the story is told it sublimates the storyteller in itself if it is really good. It turns an opinion into an idea clothed in form, colour and motion, and it converts dreams to a wealth of imagery that is frugal in its promises of actualization. The great narratives are terribly realistic for all their fantastic splendour. In the narrative, art triumphs over life and shows thereby that art is not just experience in its Sunday best, but in the flesh.

Narratives, that is, arise because their mythical content, which bears them up, is something that comes into existence on its own and quite simply would be heard through us. We cannot construct narratives. When we attempt to do so they become either allegories or hollow sounding pedagogical fables or pot boiled synopses of sequences of events that someone want to make a profit on.

Of Narratives and Leaders

The conclusion is thus that you we can never imagine a profession consisting of modern storytellers who rent out their imagination with a result that even mildly resembles the great and small stories that have given a body to passion in our culture. The chroniclers of yore, who never hid the fact that they had been hired to write the story from a given side, are no longer able to win our confidence in an age when history belongs either to the border lands of journalism which tries to approximate the scientific standards of "objectivity" that we find in our institutions of higher learning.

Totalitarian regimes have tried to come up with their own stories of where we all came from, and this now serves only as a warning. These rhetorical strategies have often gathered the content of their narratives from in one or another treasury of legends that has been handed down through the generations and which, it is claimed, establishes a lineage of "blut und boden" down to the present regime. Fortunately, as in the case of the remarkable lack of style exhibited by the Nazi regime in Germany, these attempts stand out mainly in their striking insensitivity for style and the harmonious means that distinguish the great narratives: the right to interpret them and bring into one's own life as one chooses. The inexhaustibility of this hermeneutic challenge is of course thwarted by any attempt to impose a strategy, whether out of benevolence or by the desire for power.

The closest we come to the realisation of a constructed narrative are, after all, the works of our modern epic and dramatic writers. Victor Hugo's *Les Miserables* and Henrik Pontoppidan's *Lykke-Per* are examples of successful modern myths. But they were not made to order. To be sure, there exists truly great art that was made to order, especially in music and painting, but it is very rarely the content of this work which is proscribed, even if a definite goal is often dictated—and even if the composer, like Haydn, must often wait at the table of his master, just like his other servants.

The point, then, is that it is impossible to commission narratives for particular organisations or persons that emphasise particular aspects, patterns or events in their "life", without committing rhetorical hara-kiri.

It is no less impossible to imagine a leader as someone who happily tells the story of the organizations whole without cringing.

The problem is not so much that the leader would never be able to include everything—not even statesmen do this when they account for their life and times in the biographies they in their old age, biographies that are often arabesques of not yet admitted regrets or silent

The Virtue of Leadership

prayers for justification. It is also not just here that the leader might suppress voices that would otherwise be heard. It is not even the fact that there simply is not one truth about the organization. The core of the problem, on the contrary, is that what the leader's story should stem from is the actions and events that he sets into motion.

What is decisive here is the *example*, that is, the ability of the event itself to transform itself into something that one cannot do anything but remember. It is important to remember that examples only work if they speak for themselves. If they are design to prove a particular point they accomplish the opposite. We sense both the all too good and all to evil will that resides behind a smart design. Examples can of course seduce, yes, they can seduce on the condition that they indicate that that is what they were meant to do. But then they have the goal, which is normally a short-sighted one that as soon as the first uncertain satisfaction has come about, the process of forgetting has already set in. "I want to get that man out of my hair!"

The company that despite being sure of enormous profits abandons its operations in a country that is taken over by a totalitarian regime; the company that decides not a lay off any of its employees despite pressures on the bottom line and protests from the shareholders; the company that introduces a new product and suddenly creates a whole new dimension of the world, such as was the case of Motorola rather famous little device; these are essential examples of the way to the promised creation of a good image—*if* we can be sure that the narrative is not delivered by the company itself.

Companies and institutions cannot allow themselves, as people can, to speak without having first done as they say. External and internal branding through authorized narratives can easily have a boomerang effect. There are limits to the extent to which one can stage the spontaneous and demand that we respect what has been cleverly arranged.

But there are far more legitimate ways of using narratives in a management and organizational context.

The individual employees' story of the working day, of his time spent in the company, of how he discovered a prized solution to a technical problem, or how he resolved a tight communicative difficulty. These "small stories", "narratincula", stories within stories, with their mass of biographical and incidental details are indispensable as was toward making the organization visible.

They are also the central component of any organization's dialogue, both vertically and horizontally, and they come before the discursive arguments about problems posed by such factors as production and sales. They can be understood as important shoots to a larger *we* that speaks on behalf of the community as *us*. But such spontaneously arising narratives with themes about "how we got the idea for the product that made us famous" or "the day that everyone had enough of the fact that you could never get in touch with upper management" or "the time we won over the public's suspicions that had been created by an accusation of our lack of critical reaction in regard to a regime in an overseas market" can all too easily seem like coerced or forced modulations of well-prepared themes targeting better PR.

But one has to keep in mind that these spontaneous stories do not automatically strengthen the democratic culture of a company because they can be created by groups of people who are "company types" or because they are immediately taken over by PR-people and are then shaped to conform to an ongoing project of image building and branding, which revokes the ownership of those who started it, and who must be able to recognize themselves in what is going on. The arrangement of organizational traces in experience often has a ring of totalitarianism—and is also clad in sweet and apparently justice-seeking narratives.

Add to this that the leader's legendary fear of criticism should not prevent the small, burgeoning stories from coming to the surface and becoming a part of the intellectual and emotional culture that self-assertive authorities in regard to the release of the passions of the employees claim is so important. For the story of personal conditions and functions is of course not a study of "feelings" when it works; it is rather an expression of the interplay between individual structure. Here leaders can let themselves inspired to conceive of new organizational pathways in overrun landscape. For the narrative in this sense is a little path that, like all trails in nature, also allows that one stops up and breathes freely.

A narrative can make an essential contribution to the articulation and development of the organization's *ethos*. "Ethos" is the "spirit" or "atmosphere", which is something quite particular in a company. But it is at the same time that set of attitudes, through which the organization emerges as "a little state within the state". For this reason, ethos cannot to a particular extent be established through the type of narratives that make a theme of the sovereignty of the company in the face of other companies. The egoistic winning strategies do work now and then but only in the service of a larger body, whose suit consists of a commitment to the great project that travels under the name of *humanism*.

"Humanism" is about installing the human being as the measure of things through an unconditional focus on the individual's rights and duties. To commit oneself seriously to it is supported by individual and collective formative processes because the realization of all people's opportunities in a free realm for all demands feats of social imagination. Kant's distinction in the inestimably significant little text from 1795 called *On Eternal Peace*, namely, the distinction between *the political moralist* and *the moral politician* is important here. The realisation of humanistic ideals, after all, can occur both in a rhetorical, self-righteous and thereby strategically minimalistic context (along the lines of "that must be enough for them" or "they can't appreciate it anyway") *and* in an open hearted, equitable and generous context.

The genuine leader ought to be a *moral politician*. He must at one and the same time represent his organization *and* any other human being in the whole world. This tension bears the cross of the leader: to be in engaging I a standing moral struggle with himself. His life is by no means easy as he deals with his combined roles of being squire for special interests (who disagree among themselves) and prophet for a new sense of social responsibility.

One example of the organizations humanistic engagement in relation to the narrative could be not to repress the success stories that involve the results of hiring employees with foreign names that don't immediately sound, say, American, French or German. Such an attitude is of great importance for the integration of young immigrants in the labor market, which will soon some to understand that before we once again import labor from the same cultures in the East and Middle East we should use what we already have. Fortunately, many companies have already understood this, and have begun to engage themselves actively in the battle against nationalistic and ethnic pettiness.

To be brief, organizations are not served by censoring narratives. We owe each other a new public sphere where it becomes possible to account for one's professional passions and for their often sorry institutional conditions. Narratives can, as clear documentation of the professional's good will *despite* political and administrative bulwarks contribute to reinvigorating the concept of "politics".

I thus believe that the leader must be very thorough in his effort to create a *free space for narratives* in the organization—and sometimes even a free space *from* narratives.

Such a free space allows for a *shared conversation about justice*, for it of course this that each of the individual stories are about: have we met the recognition we expected? Has attention been paid to us and have we been treated with respect? Were we allowed to do what we wanted?

No organization can accept that its members' experiences are repressed. The manager, just like the king in the fairy tales, has a duty to listen to the poorest and the lowliest of his subjects, even if he can't disguise himself as one of them. For the organization is no stronger than its weakest voice.

Chapter 12

On Presence in Organizations

A. On the Inner Logic of Presence

The concept of "presence" is becoming something of a buzzword, and that's a shame. The haste and pressure that many of us experience in our work, and sadly also in our private lives, makes the idea of presence attractive at first pass. It is in the nature of the case that the concept then becomes more than a suggestive code word; it also becomes vague. Let us therefore analyse it in greater detail because it contains a series of senses that are of enormous value for organizations and, not least, for the leader.

The concept has clear religious, theological and cosmological-philosophical connotations.

For Plato, "presence", "parousia", meant the way in which the eternal appears in time. This sense is strengthened by the Greek "epifania", which is used to describe the way the god reveals himself to us and, in Christianity of the appearance of Christ. A more profane Greek philosophical concept is offered by "hyparxis", which is the word that is translated into "existential", our concept of "existence", "that something is".

Presence, then, has this spectrum of philosophical and theological senses that in part express the possibility of meeting the eternal in time as direct personal experience if one is able to stand firm in the moment, and in part expresses one's confidence in the fact that the divine has a place among us.

In Christianity, the Greek concept of "kenosis", "das Knechtwerdens Gottes", as Luther said, i.e., the fact that God shows himself in the humblest of all forms, is absolutely central to the understanding of Jesus. In accordance with this, Søren Kierkegaard also invoked the content covered by the concept of "condescension". This means the meeting between the eternal and the timely in Jesus' person, "god in time". The concept expresses a middle ground between "immanence", "the inherent", the world as the some of all that is the case, of what we actually experience, and nothing more; and "transcendence", that which lies beyond experience.

Presence, then, in its first and fundamental sense, is God's gift to humanity, the transgression of "the guile of infinity". In Jewish mysticism, the Cabala, the word "shekinah" as mentioned earlier means the halo that surrounds the divine human and or the human divinity. Presence is here bound to a cautious attentiveness to each second of life: it becomes the expression of a personal "program", in which it is the little things that count because each of them can hide the very greatest thing. Not a single moment must be wasted. Presence here is a concept that spans from mystical experiences to the maintenance of liberty through the trivial—something which is of course also cultivated in Buddhism.

If we pull the concept of "presence" out of the cosmological context and into a philosophical context, the question becomes whether presence also can be a gift we give to each other and to ourselves.

The answer to this question is one of the major themes of existential philosophy, the philosophy that was inaugurated by Søren Kierkegaard but was first actualized as a movement a hundred years later with Martin Heidegger, Jean-Paul Sartre (and a great many other thinkers) and along with Danish philosophers like K. E. Løgstrup and Johannes Sløk.

Put simply, existentialism as a philosophical perspective rests on a basic assumption that we can at any time take our lives into our own hands. We can take our attitude toward life up for revision and we can transform ourselves. The *attitude* that serves as a basis for this choice and which had been developed by various schools devoted to the philosophy of life in the Hellenistic period—namely, the stoics and the epicureans—proceed from the concept of "to ef' hemin", "to have something in one's power". We have our lives in our power, if we want it, in the sense that we can put ourselves beyond that which happens by accident by directing our lives towards the essential. When we understand how to distinguish between that which we can really change, namely, our attitude, and over which we have no influence, which are a good many events, then we learn to feel *eudymia*, happiness about everything that happens to us.

This attitude is then understood as the (re)conquest of *presence*. By this means we become present in our lives down to the last detail because we have a "project" that implies making full use of the life we have been given. It is important to note that the German philosopher Martin Heidegger construed this presence through the concept of "Sorge", which means "care". It is of Greek origin, and when "epimeleia" was later translated into Latin as "cura" we begin to the see the breadth and intensity of the concept. It comes to mean taking responsibility for everything because one takes responsibility for one's own life upon oneself. For he that really takes responsibility for living life as a master in his own house becomes the protector of all other life. We saw in the first chapter that Plato also believed this attitude of "epimeleia" was important for leadership. This concern that begins with oneself as a confrontation with one's own relationship to death, which all schools of practical philosophy, or "philosophies of life" also develop, from Zen Buddhism to the existential therapy of Victor Frankl and Medard Boss. The key is to mean it sincerely and execute it thoroughly "by oneself" as a commitment to other people and to everything that lives.

The existential program of being "on" at all times, as one might say today, had not generally been oriented within a Christian context in the previous century nor, unfortunately, has it always been oriented by humanistic values. Existential thought has intertwined with the fascist conception of authenticity. This applies in those cases where existence is understood in complete isolation from God, without any pre-given meaning, completely finite and therefore completely beholden to the will of the individual. It also applies in cases where existence is ties to an unconditional obedience to the great secret of life, whether this be the riddle of being or the fate of a people—all these facets can be found in Martin Heidegger's works. But these thoughts can no longer be tied to proto-fascist ideologies in the form that they have been handed down to us today; rather, they are deeply integrated in the concept of human responsibility.

The existential concept of presence indicates two poles of the way of being in the world. The first is founded in an unconditional commitment to one's own life, and is tied to the religious point of view in the works of thinkers like Kierkegaard, but is also realizable outside this context, as we have seen in the work of Sartre. The other pole shows us a disingenuous and strategic way of being "present".

If we draw a horizontal line, we can put presence as a reflexive attitude to life on one pole: I carefully observe my attitude with the aim of making it more intense in its capacity to be aware of everything. I have thus chosen a way of taking my life upon myself, whether I believe that it has been given to me by God or as merely arisen as fact of my biological embodiment:

      Genuine presence   Disingenuous presence

The Virtue of Leadership

Between these two poles we find an enormous grey area, where most of us live. Even one who cultivates a deep existential commitment will of course now and the succumb to disingenuous presence. Presence, then, is the result of a process, in which I am continuously giving myself the task of being present in my life and therefore of being present *for* and *with* others.

Kierkegaard's line would look like this:

| aesthetic | ethical | religious |
| presence | presence | presence |

But there is another aspect of presence, which must be mentioned here, and which often participates in the way we use the concept.

Here "presence" means something like a "merger with one's self".

The present person manages periodically to dissolve the distance he has to himself, that is, to rescind the reflexivity that his existential commitment stems from. We can also say that we become so good at being present that we come to do so effortlessly.

This sense of presence is woven into our vague ideas about the relationship between body and soul and, as such, has little to do with existential living as an "ideal". It exists regardless of whether we describe it from the side of consciousness or from the side of consciousness, whether we "speak off the cuff" or "our fingers do the typing" (without our thinking about it), or note how "time flies when you're having fun", etc. We might also carry out an exercise from the world of Butoh dancing: swinging our arms as we walk and maintaining and open, unfocused view of things. A lot of snake oil has been distilled out of this ideal in popular books about psychology, religion, natural science and pseudo-philosophy, but it is a fact that human beings have several ways of being present that do not presuppose being constantly conscious of it—that is, permanent reflexivity.

Plato called this state of consciousness "hesyche", peace of mind, and it has many names in philosophy "apathi", "ataraxia", "Gelassenheit", but it is deeply rooted with the phenomenon of "attention", "prosoché", which the stoics in particular trained themselves in. The Roman philosopher Epictetus, who drew his inspiration from the stoics, emphasized in this chapter "On Attention" in Book IV of his *Discourses* that people are far too inclined to slacken their demands on themselves for constant attentiveness to the genuine, hat is, only to obey God and thereafter themselves, that is, only to focus on what is in accord with morality, and which expresses the relationship that I can myself master. Since one cannot master the accident and death, it is outside the sphere our concerns here. But

> *... we must remember who we are, and what is our designation, and must endeavour to direct our actions, in the performance of our duties, to meet the possibilities of our social relations.*

and

> *Is it possible to be free from fault altogether? No, that cannot be achieved, but it is possible, ever to be intent upon avoiding faults. For we must be satisfied, if we succeed in escaping at least a few faults by never relaxing our attention.*[10]

Seneca has a passage in his treatise *On Clemency,* which brilliantly illustrates the meaning of the concept of "peace of mind".

> *So we must investigate what it takes for the soul to move effortlessly in the same rhythm, have a positive attitude and look with joy upon itself, and without a occasioning a crack in this happiness, and remain in a peaceful state, neither puffed up nor depressed. For this can be called peace of mind (equitas animi).*

With the phrase "move effortlessly in the same rhythm", Seneca is evoking the stoic conception of a happy life, "euroia biou", "the gentle flow of life". But this flow is clearly conceived in terms of an *ethos*. The source is a spiritual commitment. It is *not* a state that one can attain through arbitrary techniques, including a cornucopia of attempts to force the body to the limits of its performance—here it is consciousness that counts.

Diogenes Laertius, who is our main source of stoic philosophy, says of "the gentle flow of life":

> *Again, this very thing constitutes the virtue of the happy man and the smooth current of life (euroian biou) of life, when all actions*

---

[10] Epictetus. *The Discourses*, vol. II, chap. XII. Transl. by W. A. Oldfather. Loeb Classical Library. London: Harvard University Press, 1996, p. 427 and 429.

promote the harmony of the spirit dwelling in the individual man with the will of him who orders the universe.[11]

It is therefore all important that the presence that consists in the ability to realize an inner harmony, and which seems to be solely about oneself, can only be realized *in the presence of others*.

Presence depends on an ethos, a moral and ethical will to realize one's own life.

Presence is uninteresting if it is about forgetting oneself in one's own company. The entertainment industry adopts this ideal in its image of the isolated consumer of the "real" or fictive lives of other people on the screen, but it has nothing to do with the depth of presence in its directedness and commitment to other people.

Meditation is no doubt healthy, but it is only indirectly social because it is by no means certain that the act of doing nothing is this particular and contrived way turns us into better people, and we are here talking about *being present* as a way of breaking out of your bubble.

Presence, then, cannot be discussed in terms of the isolated idea of a fusion of body and soul. We must, instead, focus upon the *reflexive mood* that is the core of true presence, and whose appropriate mental capacity is an attentiveness to oneself and to others, which is on the main rather difficult. There are no psychological or hypnotic shortcuts to paradise.

This is, not least, the reason that I must conclude that *presence is awareness of the event*.

Presence is shaped around a meeting that is encapsulated in a situation, and which it is our collective task to transform into an event. Regardless of its size or relative weight, it is to make a difference in our own life and in the lives of others.

Presence, in other words, is very much given to us by others.

We can therefore draw a vertical line:

The others

The community

The individual subject

---

[11] Diogenes Laertius. *Lives of Eminent Philosophers.* Book VII (Zeno). Transl. by R. D. Hicks. Loeb Classical Library. London: Harvard University Press, 1996, Book VII. 88-89, p. 197.

We can on this background say that the distinction between genuine and disingenuous presence also includes a distinction between good and evil presence, between a generous and a strategic form of presence. Evil, tactical and strategic presence is expressed as an attitude in *seduction*. For the seducer feels not joy in the freedom of the other, not to mention the other in himself. Only his own power brings him joy, even if he has an arsenal of good excuses, just like the political moralist. And if he appears pitiful, like a seducer who needs another to affirm him, then he is still just a seducer or a salesman that hasn't yet determined his segment.

The opposite of seduction is well grounded argumentation that understands itself as a stage in an interminable dialogue. Søren Kierkegaard has already analyzed the perversions, aversions, and diversions of the seducer, so I will not go into it here.

It is fundamental that when we transfer these conceptual distinctions to the world of organizations then we can distinguish seduction as that "practice" which it is the task of presence to rescind. Seduction leads only to short-term success and can never constitute the basis the basis of a serious leadership practice—even if we are fed this sort of nonsense all the time. Seduction is about presupposing that the other human being can be a means to satisfy one's desire, and at the same time to be so narrow minded as to be unable to understand that the whole project is a boomerang: the seducer himself ends up as a means in his own psychopathological practice. Even if he rubs his hands with glee over the fact that so many now consume his awful poisons (his merchandise) he ends up having to swallow them himself in order to maintain the illusion of their high quality. Good leadership, on the other hand, is nothing other than precisely what it *is*. It needs no stylish wrappings, profound introductions or superior rationalizations after its over. The basis of presence is the conquest of the strategies of aesthetics on a foundation of good will, thorough self-reflection, professional mastery and no mean portion of humility.

The good leader is in this sense always a student of Kant: every human being is a goal in itself, never a means. This, along with "the golden rule" constitutes the basis of any organizational practice.

B. Of Presence and Rhetoric

The greatest challenge to presence is rhetoric.

The event is *the* problem of rhetoric. No matter how consciously one attempts to plan a meeting between employees, with collaborative partners, with the management group, with people from the public sphere, etc. one never anticipate what happens. Rhetoric supposes that one can do a run through of what will happen, and that one prepare to thoroughly that one will be able to form what happens even it should be the unexpected. Rhetoric focuses on the *logos* of discourse: that which is said, the theme, content and aim of the conversation; it focuses also on *pathos*, on the emotions and passions that are shared by the parties to the conversation, and thereby on their intentions and their overt and covert interests. Finally, rhetoric addresses the *ethos* of discourse. It concerns itself with the character, personality, attitude and integrity of the speaker. This perspective implies that rhetoric is a double sided affair. There is a proper and an improper side of rhetoric.

But logos, pathos and ethos cannot be mastered. Ethos is always a wild card because he that would move others by his own integrity must have shaped himself in the image of the good, and that takes time. Or he can run into people who are so cynical and superficial that they, at least at the outset, can destroy the communicative immediacy that an ethos always works by means of: the ability to appeal to shared norms as if one was a member of a community.

It is, in other words, all about finding a balance between wanting to decide for others and surrendering to them, between manipulation and sincerity. This balance is something everyone must achieve for himself.

The key word is "duration". In Latin "duratio" is a variant of "praesentia", one way of appearing as a moment in opposition to the non-existent now. For where the now is always already past or not yet future, the moment is pure presence.

In the meeting that has a presence our words must be able to linger in the air between us.

Presence is in this sense not the opposite of haste; it is the opposite of forced haste, of rushing around. Presence can easily be reconciled with agendas; yes, a good meeting is one where the agenda is continually present as the final goal of the day.

But just as my words must linger in the air, that is, just as they must be able stand forth and remain hanging, just for a moment, before they are absorbed into the worlds of the others, so too must I be able to do the same with theirs: what they say must stand still before me.

Presence as a way of running a meeting is in other words about something as apparently banal as being able to listen.

Listening is only a serious activity if one gives oneself the time one needs to sense the attitude that lies behind was has been said. It is about being willing to guard the other's secret.

The present leader thus listens in such a way as to convince us that he is not listening in order to listen but in order learn something. At the end of the day, such an attitude is only receives provisional confirmation in the meeting itself. If it was seriously meant, then this must become apparent in action.

We are often encouraged to "lead by variety" and this is makes sense if understood in terms of the fact that companies are in need of many different perspectives all at once when they confront a kaleidoscopic environment. But the ideology of variety becomes seduction as soon as the employees no longer feel that what they say with sincerity leads anywhere or is forced into a project that the leader had planned in advance.

Presence thus involves an acute awareness of and serious interest in the other's person and opinion.

But the acute awareness of the leader could also have the effect of increasing the collective level of awareness.

Presence presupposes that the people one is present to will themselves be present. This requires trust of a social and professional kind.

Sincerity and honesty are not necessarily the same things. *Honesty* expresses a diversionary tactic, on that is a reaction to someone else's initiative. But sincerity is itself a way of beginning. Honesty admits to something or brings something into play because things were not presented as they were. Sincerity does not recognize even the possibility of its opposite: deceit. It simply does engage in the strategic games of truth and falsity because it fundamentally rests on the idea that we owe each other everything.

Sincerity, then, mercilessly exposes the sincere person. But this does not make him weak. On the contrary, it lands him in an impossible situation halfway between maximal reflexive awareness of everything that is happening *and* the ability to go straight to the heart of the matter without frills.

One who is sincere is also of the event. He understands what is happening, follows it as long as he can, tries to meet it halfway but also allows it catch itself, and turns upon it with all his might when it is about to slip through his fingers. That is why he also knows when he has reached the limits of his influence. The sincere person means *yes* when he says *yes* and *no* when he says *no*.

To be present is to be ready and willing to listen. But it also contains the other side of listening: the command.

A command in our context is a decision that is used by the one who makes it to maintain his sincerity.

The Virtue of Leadership

You can almost see it: He puts his body on display to those who are on hand by drawing their eyes to him without turning them away. He pulls everybody else's world to him and lets them bead off of him. This, however, brings them into play, albeit only on the condition that he exposes himself. He becomes, as the myths have shown us, at once king and victim, immune and vulnerable.

Being present obviously also means being the one who is prepared to be seen by everyone. You have to dress the part, and there must be fiber in the fabric. Sincerity ensures that this is the case.

One who is present is thus at one and the same time everyone's mirror and the darkness that extinguishes any image. For a true presence is strong. For he has once and for all resolved with himself why he does what he does.

This does not mean that he can't again and again waver in his faith in his choices nor that he can't show others that he does so. The fact that he admits to his dilemmas does not impugn his position because he stands by the task he has taken upon himself.

It should go without saying that this task must be in accord with the criteria for being human, for being good and just. For insofar as the task cannot pass such a test, it becomes either an example of the leader's or the organization's beginning untrustworthiness, or it becomes a technically defined project, that always proceeds on the background of a functionalistic agenda, which trains and directs our presence. Such projects must also, of course, be carried through, and they demand their own presence in the form of professional attentiveness. But even the narrowly defined technical project is also about other people. They may be able to accept being means to the project's ends in the short term but it will be the leader's ability to establish a "together" in the long haul that will determine his success. Where technical criteria of proficiency are decisive in many situations, and in the sense that it sets standards between people, such criteria are only applicable to human abilities, that is, to knowledge and skills that are born by living persons. If the leader were to separate the skill from the person he would set his organization back fifty years, to the last spasms of Taylorism, to the sort of organizational strategy that divides the work process into small portions in order to be able to proscribe their execution with the help of standardized movements and stopwatches.

It is the way in which the leader approaches other people and the various communities that is the last word in the recognition he receives in return.

The leader is bound to being available to others in a way that, almost before it has begun, can be detected as the color tone of the event to come.

C. Presence and the Event

The leader fosters meetings on the basis of planned and spontaneously arising or forced situations, and from here events grow forth.

The leader can seek to form this event or the series of events that are involved by being *directly* on hand within them. Here his own presence is of central importance, that is, the way he speaks and the way he listens, the look in his eye and on his face. But he can also seek to be *indirectly* present. This option is among leaders who are highly place in the organization. They have no way of keeping an eye on the way their decisions, suggestions and orders are executed. Indirect presence becomes the norm also because leaders must give up on the idea of engaging in a close inspection of much of the work that is carried out in the organization. The must have confidence in the capacity of their employees, their uprightness and their commitment.

In the last instance, with the delegation of tasks and, not least, whenever we are dealing with the need to believe in the employee's attitude toward the work, the strength of presence must be replaced with relationship of mutual trust.

Real trust implies that the leader can act as though *he was present in person.*

It is obvious that control through indirect presence demands a great deal of the leader unless the organization in so rigorously structured and shaped by advanced control systems that the employees can't do anything other than imagine that the leader is watching. This type of organization is no longer relevant given the sorts of production processes we know of today and is, in any case, hardly possible, not even in the military, where it had previously been so dominant. But contractual strategies that still govern the way departments control their processes are only a provisional solution that exists only for lack of alternatives because control through quantifiable objectives (number of employees involved, time of task completion, etc.) blocks the development both of the employees themselves and the quality of task execution, not to mention the way it blocks innovative initiatives. Because when the quality of one's work is being controlled down to the last detail, one naturally uses the relation between what is measured and the measured result to maintain appropriate levels of resources, even where it is unnecessary, and to maintain positions of power, precedence and custom, and, of course, to protect the grey area where freedom unremarkably mixes with sloth.

The question then arises: How should the leader behave on a daily basis in order to be present even when he is not there?

The answer is simple, even if it is difficult to realize in practice. He must be so present that he sets his stamp on his surroundings. He must mark them, so that they may "mark" him, even when he is not there.

We can compare this condition with the facts pertaining to a string quartet.

Before a performance one practices perhaps forty times. Each these rehearsals the leader constantly intervenes, both by making comments and by defending his musical idea when others challenge it. But when the moment of performance arrives, the leader can no longer correct and direct. He cannot even scream and shout from the sidelines. The only thing he can do is nod to start and end the performance, and to use his face, his body and his foot to emphasize the dynamics of the piece. There is no way around it. This is when it counts.

But the presence that is finally replaced by trust can only be replaced insofar as it happens in relation to a "spirit" or "ethos" that has been built up – or at least strengthened – through the daily practice of the organization and the leader. Such an ethos is intangible. It cannot just be conjured up, not to mention constructed.

So we must therefore close with the question: Is there a technique of presence?

Such "techniques of presence", after all, would consist in organizational strategies or educational initiatives, learning programs.

It is here very important to be careful. One must not believe that just because one gets a chance to use one's body in the context of various courses, where one for example plays meditating Indian on the hillsides in pine forests, or shamans dance around one on the ice, or because one forces oneself to eat a meal completely naked, that one will thereby get close to presence. Actors have a series of techniques that allow them to move about freely, conscious of their own body, and of the way others perceive it, and conscious of intonation and gesture, in short, they speak "with presence". But such techniques can easily come off as being contrived in the real the world where they are uncommon, for one thing, and, for another, seem artificial when they become ordinary.

We will not here run through all the technologies of presence that are on offer today. I will simply claim that the only experience that can generally strengthen presence is the conversation—with others and with oneself.

We know that we can spin the actions of a mediocre politician on the screen so that he becomes a hit, at least for a time. But we also know that no leader can in the long run control his spin. Events that build on a meeting between that a physically on hand can only in a very limited sense be scripted and staged. This is owed to the fact that their theme is thought and the feelings that accompany thoughts. These, precisely, *accompany* them, but they can neither create nor replace them.

This is serious business.

Chapter 13

Strategy and Freedom

To complete the picture of the new leadership in both the public and the private spheres we must treat the concept of "strategy". The consequence of what has been written so far is that the concept of "strategy" can no longer retain its traditional sense.

In ordinary language, the words "strategy" and "politics" will cover the same meaning when "politics" is about finding the most effective means to reach a given goal, though the goals need not be clarified beforehand. The meaning of the concept "strategy" only distinguishes itself here from the meaning of the concept "politics" by implying also a sense of what can be planned more systematically because it can apparently be carried out without insurmountable obstacles. "Politics" will generally also be able to refer to longer term perspectives and action plans that have are broader and more ideologically clear intention, but this is not always the case. If the concept is used pejoratively about all activities that puts the means before the ends and which operate if not haphazardly then cynically, then they mean more or less the same. Von Clausewitz' famous maxim that "war is the continuation of politics by other means" fits well into this identification of politics and strategy.

Despite this, it is possible to discern a meaning of "politics" that connects it with something thoroughly positive, with attitudes that transgress narrow interests and which have a clear sense of the role that strategy or tactics—which is to say, different communicative ways to use one's power—can even play. From this perspective the leader main task can also be seen as "political".

The move that makes the application of this perspective to the leadership of organizations (and not just on the leadership of states) a relatively uncomplicated matter to is the conscious application of the *metaphor of the state society* to private and public ventures.

I am here referring to the survey of metaphors that guide business administration in the next chapter, but I will treat the metaphor of the state society also in what follows here.

The use of this metaphor is justified by appeal to current developments in history where private businesses have sought to stand out in the public sphere as agents whose actions are founded in a homogenous organizational reality and who understand themselves as responsible to the society that provides them with their market. The target here is finally global: a world society. This new attitude toward the market, which must pass from a national to a global public sphere, has itself been made necessary by the intensification of the publicity that is bestowed upon all social action, which the increasing competition over "lifestyle" and "image" has brought. The internet has made it difficult for businesses to operate in the dark. For as soon as they are discovered, their merits and demerits are laid bare by the new guardians of economic morality. When strategies intended to cordon off a segment of the market fail the company is left to whole of the public sphere where it has to sell its wares to people who assess them on the basis of factors like the regimes that supply its raw materials and the way the animals that have given their bodies to the production process have lived. The organization must therefore itself perform like a little state within the state, understood in terms of its relation to its "citizens" (employees), to other "states" (the additional private and public organizations), to the "federal structure" (the national market) and the "global structure" (the world society). All these relations must be able to see the light of day. Our metaphorical approach is therefore more than justified.

As has already been mentioned several times, there exists a little inestimable philosophical masterpiece from 1795, the historical importance of which has been enormous. Immanuel Kant's *On Eternal Peace* can supply us with an abundance of metaphorical analogies for the task that we must now undertake: to rethink the concept of strategy for organizations in terms of a *normative politics* as a basis for leadership in organizations.

In a supplement to this the first part of this work, which delineates the maxims that make eternal peace possible, Kant presents a series of reflections about the relation between the *political moralist* and the *moral politician*, which are highly suited to distinguish the leader that uses values-based management strategically from the leader that take ideals and norms seriously.

But let us first connect Kant's conceptual domain with the aforementioned arguments for the fact that the company *must* stand out through more than aesthetic image management and rhetorical branding. For Kant emphasises through two maxims that *the public*, in the sense of a perfectly open sphere where all actions *and* its motives are known to all is the litmus test of politics with moral integrity.

All those actions that pertain to the rights of others and whose maxims [basis for action] are not compatible with complete publicity are false. (p. 449)

And

All those maxims that need full publicity (in order not to miss their mark) are in accord with the unification of law and politics. (p. 453)

That's straight talking. The company whose personnel policies, or HRM strategies, cannot stand full disclosure does not respect the individual employee. And only the product and service strategy that *can* give good reasons for its own existence and therefore in its form and content (materials, procedures) deserves the labels "socially responsible" and "sustainable". It is a scandal that food products in the EU do not have to be labeled where genetic technologies have been employed in their production and that it is instead only permitted to indicate these technologies when they have not been employed.

But because Kant's maxims are so uncompromising, they also show how difficult it is for private companies to live up their own signals about social responsibility. For what is private is of course "private" precisely in the sense of "not public". Even if legislative practice is opening up in these times in regard to the iron fisted protection of a corporations right to hide large portions of its activities and to demand the right to knowledge developed on its grounds, it running a business remains tied to a lengthy series of arguments for the need for a threshold of information between the private and public spheres. This means that the company's way of stepping into the public sphere is guided by selective mechanisms that are strategic and tactical in nature.

But it is an open question whether secrecy is necessary for the preservation of private initiative beyond the area of production. The need for secrecy in regard to corporate stocks is only "necessary", it would seem, because the system hides something that could not survive the light of day. If the content and extent of property cannot stand being publicly known, what, then, is it that is undemocratic about property rights?

This whole circus around the confidentiality and publicity of information that is enacted in discussions about information that pertains to the value of stocks, or the about the right of the state to gather full information about the techniques of production is put into relief by Kant's pointed remark:

> *Even if the sentence honesty is the best policy contains a theory that sadly all too often stands in opposition to practice, the corresponding theoretical sentence, honesty is better than all politics far more illustrious beyond any all objections, yes, it is the inexorable condition of the first. (p. 437-8)*

We already have a clear image of the new, normative leader. Honest is never a strategy to him. He can resist the temptation that any application of values, ideals and norms in an organization always involves: to say one thing and do something else; or to do something and either justify it with false motives after the fact, trivialize the effort afterwards or ally himself with interest groups that benefited from the action (such as the stock holders)—these are strategies that Kant deals with in detail. The disingenuous leaders "god" is "bonus eventus" (the good event)—the action that is a success when seen from the point of view of the bottom line, even if it does not live up to the rest of the company's set of norms (p. 441-2).

The ground, then, is prepared for an immersion in the fruitful distinction between the "moral politician" and the "political moralist"—between the leader who means what he says and does what he has provided moral reasons for, on the one hand, and the leader that does what his tactical and strategic cunning and sense for the situation determines to be most profitable, and thereafter justifies it by appeal to one or another form of necessity afterwards. This could be the state of the market, the exchange rate, the good of the stock holders, the demands of the board or the employees' lack of skill.

The leader we are trying to picture here is expressed with crystalline clarity in the following sentence of Kant's, which may have targeted against the most powerful potentate of his own time (Frederick the Great of Prussia), but which full well applies to the modern leader, if he is to have power[12]. Kant says:

> *The moral politician will make this his basic axiom: when first defects in the constitution of the state or the relation between states*

---

[12] Volker Gerhardt provides a discussion of which dukes Kant had in mind, and his ambivalence in regard to Frederick the Great, in his excellent book on Kant's *On Eternal Peace*, entitled *Immanuel Kants Entwurf Zum ewigen Frieden. Eine Theorie der Politik*, Darmstadt: Wissenschaftliche Buchgesellschaft, 1995.

> have arisen, which one could not have prevented, then it is a duty, especially for the heads of state, to give thought to how they, as soon as possible, can be rectified and be brought into accord with natural right, as it provides an example before our eyes by virtue of the idea of reason; this also if it should sacrifices of self love. (p. 441)

The good leader, in other words, must set universal reason over his own interests. He must set the moral above the technical (p. 444). He must choose the "wisdom of the state" over the "cleverness of state", in the moment of truth, even if he must also possess political cunning in order to participate in politics in the first place. Kant is never in any doubt about this. Politics presupposes experience; its concrete actions cannot be deduced from maxims. You can neither work out a political solution by reason alone nor learn it in advance. But this does not exclude the standing excuse that one can avoid giving thought to one's own cleverness in moral terms, since moral shoddiness is a boomerang. Shoddy motives always expose themselves in the end.

> Thus true politics can never take a step without rendering homage to morality. Though politics by itself is a difficult art, its union with morality is no art at all, for this union cuts the knot which politics could not untie when they were in conflict. The rights of men must be held sacred, however much sacrifice it may cost the ruling power. One cannot compromise here and seek the middle course of a pragmatic conditional law between the morally right and the expedient. All politics must bend its knee before the right. But by this it can hope slowly to reach the stage where it will shine with an immortal glory. (p. 448)

The universe of Kant's thought is foreign to business administration and at the same time exceedingly close because the world of business consists of people who love freedom. Even if the larger part of economic theory generally justifies its actions in a utilitarian context, that is, grounds the justice of that which happens in the individual's ability to extract joy from it, this picture is beginning to dissolve. Kant's ideas about "formal normativity" that is not oriented by the subjective quality of experience, that is, in terms of goals that are contingent in relation to the community, but in terms of the ability to live according to maxims *is* the only way to articulate a pure normativity:

Act in such a way that your maxim can be a universal law (the goal is of no consequence). (p. 444)

This is the clearest expression of duty.
But duty requires freedom.

So it is, for example, a basic proposition for moral politics that a people unites solely through the rightful principles of freedom and equality and this principle is not justified through cleverness, but through duty. (p. 445)

For this reason the concept of "freedom" must, if seen from a legal point of view, not be defined as "being able to do what one wants so long as one does not violate the freedom of another" but rather "the ability not to obey outer laws other than those that I have given my consent to" (p. 416).

This "competence"—the German word is "Befugnis" and it means also "certification", "authority" and "right"—can also be seen as the basis of the hypermodern organization. The possibility of active, conscious consent that has been properly thought through, which is built into Kant's definition of outer freedom (the inner consists in the ability to follow a maxim beyond one's own subjective desires), but nonetheless consent that accepts a respect for the community is the condition under which the organization can survive because this consent imply that the employees can experience that they have themselves committed to it.

We must now ask: What sort of power in organizations is compatible with the ideals of a moral politics (strategy) and with the ideals of maximum individual freedom *when organizations at the same time demand loyalty that is more than formal*, that is, a question of blood, sweat and tears.

For Kant, this problem seems obviously connected with a representative, republican constitution, that is, with a democracy of enlightened, well-educated citizens. The word "republic" today means simply a state constitution that is "free", that is, not connected with a monarchy, or it refers, not least through American history, to a political tradition that emphasizes local autonomy over centralized, federal power. The republican constitution is not necessarily democratic but it presupposes a separation of powers into executive and legislative branches. Kant, in fact, gives us the possibility of discussing the relation between strong leadership and representation because the majority of private companies, like the majority of public organizations, are today "republican dictatorships". But Kant seems to believe that a broad, democratic version of the republican constitution is not necessarily connected with the strength of representation, at least not as an whole, because the oppositions within the organization will just be projected upwards into its higher echelons and create inefficiency. Visible and strong leadership confronts the organization with itself, with its freedom, with its prison walls, with its impractical limitations and with its potential strength in its "spirit".

We can without exaggeration emphasize that organizations in these years are experiencing a process that certain European states experienced two hundred years ago, namely, the transition from despotic to republican dictatorships.

This analogy raising the question of how the organization can solve the problem of representing everyone's interests, which is the basis of the republican constitution.

Or, said differently, it raises the question of what the application of the metaphor of the state society in its republican variant can tell us about the level of employee participation that is optimal for a hypermodern organization.

It is important, first of all, that a company neither can nor should appear as a state within the state in the sense that it might set it its own goals and make use of its own "methods" that depart from the set of norms that governs the values of the state in which it operates. The freedom of the employees will always be threatened if the company presents itself as a political agent that pursues its own interests. In such cases, the employee will be left in a dilemma between regard for the organization (his own survival within it) and his function as a citizen.

We can imagine cases where organizations represent a universal, human reason in contrast to a regime, or where organizations, whether public or private, are one step ahead of with regard to the development of a reasonable democracy, but these exceptions do not justify an organization in taking the law into its own hands.

When we look at the strategies of large, multinational corporations, we often find terrifying examples of what Kant calls "the antinomies between politics and morals". There is here talk of actions that characterize the political moralist, which justifies his will to power when it is satisfied through apparently "rational" norms. When companies are incorporated in the firm through buyouts, one often refers to "the interests of the consumer" or "the economies of scale"; or one invokes "the demands of the market" or "stockholder value", both of which are apparently immune to argument. But we find just as often an appeal to pseudo-moral justifications that no one can have confidence in. One motivates an action, for example, by appeal to "quality, health and safety concerns" or "concerns about the populations of third world countries" or "about nature" (sustainability) or to "the preservation of jobs". These sorts of rationalizations are almost never presented in a well argued form. That is, they are never presented along with the explanations and data that would be able to contradict them, but hang in the air without being able to satisfy those who at least try to be critical. They are even less comforting to those that don't care anyway.

It is almost refreshing when someone dares to say it like it is: that their main concern is with the bottom line and with power.

The freedom of the employees depends on being presented with the values and "laws" of the company, which he must consent to, in such a way that he can take a critical and thorough position on them before he says "yes".

This means that there are methods and procedures in the company that make it possible for the employee to have a dignified discussion with the management about the values upon which the company is founded. The word "dialogue" is here intended to indicate that both the necessary and sufficient conditions are in place in the organization in order to ensure that the employee is fully informed. Dialogue only makes sense on the background of a *right* to information. And this, in turn, only makes sense on the background of a *duty* to acquire so much information that one cannot thereafter say that one didn't know what one's interests were.

The radical nature of this demand reduces the meaning of tools such as "ethical accounting", that are supposed to work through formal consensual processes that rarely, however, gives the individual party full freedom to move. For one thing, the values of all parties are not normally taken into consideration and, for another, management often simply excludes the values that actually involved or fails to relate them to interpretative possibilities and opportunities for application. What is most important is that is the employee's right to present values within the minor public sphere, to interpret them and to demand the leader, too, interprets them. The last demand is the most serious one because it demands that the formal values and visions are interpreted in the light of the interests of all interested parties without any "reservation mentalis", i.e., without any clever reservations and with the tricks of procurement and virtuosity in the art of arranging principles to suit the needs of the moment.

In this context, it is also decisive that the employee has a right to compare the organizations values with the set of values that governs society as a whole. This includes the right to expose minimalism in the application of values and attempts to jump the gun or cheat on the scales.

But this potential employee attitude demands a culture in which management supports its employees to the utmost degree in their attempts to learn such a practice. It does not come all by itself but must be cultivated through the interplay of education and edification—it is a *formative* process. This demands a high degree of awareness of the demands that are made of new forms of democratic education in an the knowledge society, in the information age. The leader cannot lift this task alone; it is a job for a whole community, a society. But it presupposes that greater correspondences are established between the formative process in the educational system and the formative processes that occur in businesses. Company's need their own Great Books programme, their own academies, their own public philosophers.

For it of paramount importance that the values or maxims that are articulated in organizations are met half way through an interpretative capacity of the employees that does not understand itself in purely legal terms, which is to say, in terms of precedence or formalized pragmatism, but has the stature that is needed to include the ethical and moral dimension.

We can here invoke the stoic Epictetus. In his chapter on "Freedom", from Book IV of his *Discourses*, he writes:

For this is the cause to men of all their evils, namely, their inability to apply their general preconceptions to the particular instances.[13]

The ills of man, then, stem from his lack of judgment, his inability to convert normatively reflected attitudes into the basis for *all* action.

The consequence of the employees' freedom is the opportunity for consistent support for the organization from within. A space of opportunity is opened for genuine loyalty, based in the passion that stems from critique and consent, in short, from personal authority.

---

[13] Epictetus. *The Discourses*, vol. II, chap. XII. Transl. by W. A. Oldfather. Loeb Classical Library. London: Harvard University Press, 1996, p. 257.

In this context, all management rhetoric becomes a very serious matter. Initiatives that are intended to seduce employees or markets will always have the opposite effect because autonomous people need not be seduced. Strategies of seduction in any case only express contempt for those one would seduce and, at the end of the day, contempt for oneself because one wants to rule over someone that one does not recognize.

Those companies that neither engage in branding nor cultivate their image, but set honesty above all politics, will of course send the very clear signal that they really have something to offer.

They will not, then, feel threatened by other organizations since their product or service is unique. What is unique has its own presence.

A far more radical and serious commitment to universal humanism could arise in this perspective, which has the open, morally grounded global community as its goal.

After all, it will be possible for employees to be at the same time moral persons and passionate members of the organization. There will no longer be talk of two worlds. The energy that is expended on schisms, personal dilemmas and attempts to unify politics and morality under impossible conditions will then be released for use in a collective effort to conquer the historical and cultural barriers that still inhibit the development of a humanistic global community.

This is the task that the new leader must contribute to completing.

PART V

THE NEW LANGUAGE OF LEADERSHIP

Chapter 14

The Shifting Figures of Management and Leadership

In his famous little paper "On Truth and Lies beyond Morality", Friedrich Nietzsche pointed out that our sense of what is true is guided more by hidden metaphors, created by our bodily-sensory interaction with the world, than by pure intellectual and universal reason. Ever since, philosophers, psychologists and anthropologists have focused on the way metaphors guide experience and foster knowledge. Nietzsche pessimistically pointed out that the great majority of metaphors are today worn down beyond recognition by use, a bit like the portraits on old coins.

In his *Poetics*, Aristotle understood metaphors as a function of our ability to "transfer" ("epiphora") a pictorial representation from one domain of reality to another. The state as an organism, the body as a machine, consciousness as a computer—there are lots of them, and more turn up all the time. In his *Rhetoric*, he pointed out that metaphors work especially when they evoke some kind of strangeness. But we also have to feel that they are natural, which is to say, uncontrived. That is, we must think that they are expressions whose origin we cannot fathom while at the same time finding their sensually captivating power "on the mark".

The sensitivity to the importance of the national culture for the shaping of social action that emerged in the aftershocks of the universalism of the Enlightenment was prefigured in the elegant systematicity of Humboldt's posthumous masterwork from 1836 about the spirit of language. It was entitled "On the Variety of Human Linguistic Structures and its Influence on the Spiritual Development of the Human Race". The standing grudge match between the Greek and the German languages over the right to be the best expression of thought, which had to lie dormant until Heidegger came along, was thus inaugurated by abandoning the dream of the "original language". This was the language God used when talking to himself, the language before Babel and the only surrogate for it was the Hebrew language, which was accepted as such despite widespread anti-Semitism until it found its apotheosis in mathematics, which is universal by virtue of the fact that its syntax is completely unambiguous and its "words" are either conventionally determined or empty.

The aftershocks of Humboldt's ideas could be felt in waves almost a hundred years later, in the beginning of the twentieth century, when the Sapir-Whorf thesis in linguistics articulated the idea that different kinds of language contained different versions of what Kant had thought was the universal, trans-cultural basis of all knowledge, namely, time and space. The language of the Hopi Indians contained syntactical structures that simply indicated a different understanding of time than that of the Europeans.

In the same period (ca. 1920) the Austrian philosopher Ludwig Wittgenstein wrote his famous collection of theses on the structure of the world, *Tractatus Logico-Philosophicus*. Its basic premise was that language constitutes an absolute limit for our experience and cognition. The meaning of life, then, must lie outside what can be spoken of or, rather, what is meaningful, the meaning of sense, is that which we cannot talk about.

The so-called linguistic turn in philosophy and the humanities was thereby inaugurated.

This same Wittgenstein would spend the rest of his life in the attempt to get closer to the core of the problem of the meaning of sense, but ended up articulating a program to uncover the way experience and cognition is tied to our "forms of life". These looked very much like those proposed by Humboldt. Wittgenstein's strange concept of "language games" became infinitely influential, invoking the metaphor that would govern philosophy throughout most of the twentieth century, namely, the "game".

It would fall to the German philosopher Martin Heidegger (born, like Wittgenstein, in 1889) to inform his contemporaries that the word "game", "paidia", has its Greek roots in the word "paizo", to play like a child, "pais", and that the game of life, "the world game", is not played by a god but by an innocent, not malevolent, divine child. (He presented this idea in his great essay "The Law of Sufficient Reason").

After the Second World War, the great philosophers understood that the limit of philosophy, and thereby the limit of language, consists in the language that it is bound to and thereby to the metaphors that govern that which the language is ultimately able to refer to. Since it was no longer possible for this to be a simple world, given to the senses, but was a world that only came to be in our interactions with it and which, because it had to be interpreted, became meaningful through the world of language itself, language had to be understood as both that which gave us reality and that which took it from us. Language would not put its cards on the table (to stick to the gaming metaphor) and the struggle to extract its secrets from its clasp was centered on displaying the forms through which it came to make sense. In the middle of this constellation was metaphor itself, for philosophy was of course itself a game played with language and in language and therefore in no position to claim to be beyond the language that it would have to distinguish itself from to preserve the truth. Wittgenstein took the consequences of this insight and did not publish anything after his first book, *Tractatus Logico-Philosophicus*.

The problem of understanding the language as such, the whole airy citadel of sense, was tied to the ability to reach into the historically propagated metaphors that dominate practical language use. The focus of the Oxford philosopher J. L. Austin was on language as "speech act", which reinforced the trend. But when we do something, we *act*, and when we act, we take our bodies with us. In the "logic" of the great languages, and not least within all the domain-specific languages, professional jargons, and the vocabularies organized by practical necessity, including management terminologies, a number of embodied experiences are practiced in our interaction with the world. Nietzsche was right. Language emerges from a feeling of truth that is directed toward the metaphor because it is as "close" as we get to material, sensible reality.

In the last quarter of the twentieth century, metaphor became all important in the attempts of the various special sciences to understand their own foundations, whether in order to ensure their validity or in order criticize their legitimacy. In the first case, one would claim that metaphor was a solely heuristic element, a working hypothesis of sorts that served to communicate a theoretical image of the world, which could then be confirmed by more empirical methods. In the other case, it was claimed that our scientific institutions are founded on sand because they were not able to recognize the metaphors that tacitly guided thought or because these metaphors, when recognized, turned out to be mirages, pure projections concealing the real.

In this context, where we are talking about management and leadership, we are not trying to investigate the universal status of metaphor. The aim is neither to engage in epistemology (the theory of knowledge) or ontology (the theory of being) but, on the contrary, to reach the metaphorical foundation that makes the various strategic projects within management studies and organization theory seem so relevant, enthralling and obvious to its practitioners and theoreticians.

We can here indicate a series of basic metaphors for management thinking that have prevailed since the Second World War: war, game, the theatre, sports, the church, the family, the state and the arts. If one may pardon evoking one of them, these metaphors have helped to "set the stage" for the meeting of theoretical and empirical research up til the present.

Two provisos are important to bear in mind as we develop these metaphors. First, most of these metaphors have been employed in management thinking from the very beginning, especially in work on the nature of the state, and they also appear in management theory as it was practiced between the wars. Second, a metaphor does not die as soon as another appears on the scene but old metaphors live on in new guises and participate in constellations with new metaphors in so far as the contradictions between them are not too great.

The first great metaphor in the period after the Second World War is that of rational strategy, formed in the image of the *game*. The game does not just occupy the attention philosophers and humanists but can be found also in the social sciences, where cybernetics was the godfather both of the computer and of strategic game theory. That the idea of the game has been deployed in this technical sense, however, should not blind us to its metaphorical background, the foundational metaphor of all strategic thinking, namely, *war*. Since war is legal in a capitalistic society as a form of competition, and since the last century can be understood as the victory of liberal, free market democracies over totalitarian command economies, albeit modified in local context through various versions of the welfare state and social democracy, then war is the background for the whole play of metaphor that has dominated economics and business administration ever since. This metaphor will then either, as in case of the game, express a technical approach to the progress of war or, as in the case of the remaining metaphors, express an increasing softening of the emphasis on aggression and egoism in the grand war-game of liberalism.

The perspective of game theory makes operations analysis relevant to leadership because an operation can be described as a game with certain rules, certain pieces and clear criteria for winning and losing. Operations analysis includes the idea that a field of problems can be exhaustively described in view of the parameters that are decisive for making rational decisions. That is, the goal is to draw optimal conclusions in relation to the choices and distributions of means in the hopes of achieving a given goal, or even in the hopes of deciding among a range of possible goals, as these are manifest in the light of several different criteria.

The models of game theory became still more appealing to strategically self-aware leadership when the technical evolution of the computer in 60s and 70s began to open the prospect of high speed data processing.

But during the 80s it became clear to many that models that had been derived from operations analysis have two decisive weaknesses, even in the ramified form that included choices among goals. First, the choice of parameters is highly uncertain. It is possible to overlook the most important parameters for the goals one has set oneself and it can be difficult to determine when one has taken a sufficient amount of parameters into account. Herbert Simon (a computer scientist, psychologist and economist) had an enormous impact through his Nobel Prize-winning critique of closed operations analysis, which introduced the idea of "bounded rationality". He understood that managers never make decisions in contexts that are defined by well-described parameters—they simply don't have time to do so.

A second weakness of operations analysis is that the choice of criteria relevant to one's goals are often tied to the horizon of operations analysis itself, that is, it is bounded by what it is technically capable of. Add to this the fact that operations analysis must itself operate with a very coarse and hardly especially sensitive concept of the dynamics of a situation. After all, an operations analysis is a reconstruction of an artificial decision situation on the basis of a modeled world.

Moreover, one begins to see that decisions are primarily about communication. If others become means to the attainment of given aims, whether as employees or as customers, the operations analysis will be very weak because it presupposes that people can be treated as things. But human behavior, expectations, motives, wishes and dreams cannot be quantified. The strategist must become still more strategic. He must take into account what was then called "double contingency" by Talcott Parsons, i.e., the fact that human beings react to one's intentions toward them in unintended ways. If I want to get someone to do something, I must take a roundabout route because they of course either also want to get me to do something, or they expect that I want to get them to do something and act accordingly.

The way out of this dilemma is for the leader to become a stage director. For one can get another person to do what one wants if one can get them to identify with the action of a play and the role they have been assigned. The role defines both the goals of a person's actions in a given context and the meaning of what is accomplished.

The *theatre* became the next great metaphor in the Parnassus of management theory. It became the framework of symbolic interaction, or so-called sensemaking behavior, to the advantage of the company. The theatre arguably emerged as a metaphor for the organization from the "stage" as a model of life and has thereby been an essential part of Occidental culture since Aristotle delineated the principles of the Greek theatre and Shakespeare declared that "all the world's a stage". The metaphor of the theatre was later reinforced by the orchestra as a model of the relationship between the patriarch and the employee (Marx, for example, uses this image in a positive sense as an expression of the technological necessity of management). In it is obvious that this metaphor demands the evolution of the stage itself – or the culture of the orchestra – in order to be relevant for management and leadership. The audience must become more interactive, and the conductor must become more "democratic", before these metaphors can really be made meaningful for modern management. But this does not mean that we must radically transform these metaphors. They simply need to be elaborated or refined in terms of the resources that are already embedded within them.

There are, especially, insights from anthropology, ethnology and psychology, which could be used in this context. For one thing, the ideas were produced in the US, where these disciplines dominated and where theories of strategic management triumphed. For another, these disciplines have long studied role-specific behavior in particular contexts, including social groups and therefore behavior determined by peer pressures, which complemented the evolution already taking place in the social relations within firms. Goffman's famous book from 1959, *The Presentation of Self in Everyday Life*, which used precisely the metaphor of the theatre to describe social relations turned out to have an enormous influence. Goffman applied the distinction between three aspects of presentation. First, there is a "backstage", where the role of playwright and therefore also the role of strategic planner and manager belongs; next, there is a "front stage", where the actors, i.e., the employees come and go; and, finally, there is the audience, which corresponds to the rest of the stakeholders, in particular, the customers and investors. Symbolic management came as a wave in the 1970s, drawing on analogies from social anthropology, but also, in its more advanced forms, on Ernst Cassirer's concept of the cultural significance of symbols. Certain economists began to sense already at this point that there was something to be gained, if not by cutting out the middlemen (psychology, ethnology, sociology) altogether, then at least by going directly to the source, namely, philosophy. Phenomenological philosophers like Alfred Shütz, who, like Cassirer, was originally a political refugee in the USA, for example, came to have enormous influence on the evolution of the theory of organization.

Now, it is obvious that the logic of the metaphor of the theatre is also determined by technological progress, which is accompanied by an increased emphasis on services and knowledge processes. The increasing immateriality of capitalistic products, and thereby the significance of new strategies of innovation, including what is called knowledge management, but also increasingly public services, including high levels of education, makes necessary a focus on delegation of competences, innovative initiative and responsibility. The metaphor of the theatre is apt in this context because the actor (the employee) has a space of freedom in which to interpret the script and to set himself apart, indeed, to improvise, also when the director is no longer on hand.

Since the concept of a role, like the concept of a mask, has been so decisive a part of the everyday understanding of others and oneself since the Baroque, it of course survives in all management thinking today. But the metaphor of "staging" has come to be even more important in recent years by being transferred from the art of theatre to other arts, which have always been more socially "closed", such as music and painting, and has at the same time undergone an extensive transformation to a concept of performance. Managers are today confronted with the possibility of learning to direct a choir or a string quartet; employees from two companies learn to merge by singing the same piece of choral music; improvisational forms in jazz are the theme of serious theories of organization and management; but one must be aware of the transformation that these metaphors have undergone in passing from the world of theatre. For whereas the theatre could be used as an approach to the problem of the rational governance of agents, the use of art is today about governing with a trace of structurally propagated, not to mention hierarchically shaped, control. When the plot becomes the problem, when there is no script, when there is neither sheet music nor libretto, then the leader must depend on the good will of the agents (the "actors"). It is now all about finding a "flow", that underlying stream, the "nisus", the power that smolders under the surface, and which can break through like a geyser and carry everyone down in a single paradisal swoop. In the performance arts, researchers, management consultants and leaders are now looking for methodically prepared experiences, or are, in the manner that a shaman could be proud of, trying to invoke this gesture, which contains an indeterminate but enormous directedness while it also carries the secret of the anticipatory "logic" of the unintended.

The metaphor of the theatre is also transformed through the fact that the art of rhetoric has found a place in management theories. (It has been rescued from its exile, where it served as a basis only for contemptible marketing jargon and is being given the opportunity to be associated with serious theories of communicative action.) The stage for the act of seizing power over one's audience is thereby moved outside the theatre and into ordinary life. The slide from the rhetorical to a poetics of leadership, which we see through the increasing focus on organizational narratives, expresses a setback in historical terms, a return to the mechanisms of consensus-formation that characterized pre-industrial societies. After all, the theatre is an institution that has been secularized in modern times, which is to say that, in line with the evolution of industrial society, it has lost its connection to Christian allegories of human vanity and the frailty of life.

So we can say that the focus on the metaphor of the theatre, which begins in the 1980s in the theory of management and organization, survives and proliferates wildly in accord with a new fascination with the arts in this same context. The watchword to understanding this evolution is, as already mentioned, the focus on *performance*. It is a domain of open, unpredictable and process-oriented services and management functions, which cannot be addressed through metaphors of the previous century: sports, the family, religion and the state, which had hitherto shaped the understanding of the company.

Sports may at first appear to be the least interesting metaphor because it only continues the metaphor of war in a modified form. Its focus on group solidarity, group identity, unconditional loyalty and the spirit of combat is no different than the demands made on soldiers with the important exception that death is in principle left out of the equation, both as something to avoid and something to accomplish. Only the ambiguous concept of a "coach" seems to be an original contribution from the world of sport. It transgresses the boundaries of sport itself and approaches a concept of individuality that does not, at least on the surface, belong there, but which can easily be found in philosophy. As an example, take Plato's detailed programs for the education of cultivated citizens in the *State* and the *Laws*. Here athletic training stands on par with mathematics and music with a view to fostering the development of a person that is able to discover a harmonious balance between personal development and social progress. The mutual ambiguity inherent in the related concepts of "coach" and "mentor", between being ways to personal liberation and means to develop one's ability to demonstrate loyalty toward an organization or the community, indicates this harmonic tension. It also indicates the fact that education in the arts of war and therefore the maintenance of the body's strength and health was a duty of citizenship in the Greek world *and* a duty to oneself. The road to personal edification through sport thus passed through collective duties for the Greeks while it is today confused by the chimera of modern sports, an existence that oscillates between natural play and deadly, professional seriousness. One must not forget that Socrates had been an ordinary soldier and many of his interlocutors in Plato's dialogues were athletes or officers.

The problem is that, while learning and self-knowledge can to some extent occur within the framework of a vague military metaphor and by reference to the world of sport, with its emphasis on "overcoming oneself", the very act of relating it to a serious notion of getting an education in the humanities can quickly lead to a fundamental conflict. This conflict is beginning to emerge in business today when coaching and mentoring come to be about the liberation of the person from the role and not just about facilitating the integration of the individual in the team. It is a tension between coaching as a dialogue that could end with a change of job, trade or even a whole life, and thus the exposure of subjective obstacles to entering into particular forms of work and particular communities.

The three foregoing metaphors—games, war and sports— resemble each other by the fact that they are all about leadership through a form of legitimacy that is meticulously specified by the institutional structure of the phenomenon itself and which can therefore foster unconditional loyalty, that is, leadership on the basis of values that one can presuppose that the employee has accepted in advance and which can therefore be relatively straightforwardly invoked as a basis of sanction. But the *church* and the *family* as metaphors of organization are arranged on the opposite side because values are not negotiated here but express unconditional behavioral, emotional and logical rules, which are grounded in a fundamental, institutional and non-negotiable authority. This holds regardless of whether we are talking about a church, a society, an organization or a group. *The State Society* as a metaphor, by contrast, implies that the employee has freely given consent to aspire to these values. This, of course, is something that democracies only have to a certain extent in relation to the constitution, to stick with the metaphor.

This difference between metaphors is reinforced further by the fact that the metaphors of both religion and family do not distinguish between work and leisure. The company that functions in the manner of a "church" or as a "family" does not give any space of freedom for its members. The state metaphor, by contrast, does have such a space of freedom. It emphasizes that membership in an organization on the basis of free choice is a commitment that applies only within its walls. Beyond these walls, however, there is a space of relative freedom so long as one honors the contract. (One must, for example, to a certain degree treat the knowledge one has produced there as the property of the organization. But even this norm is beginning to dissolve as ever more frequent changes of job make it impracticable.) One should also be able, at least at times, to function as an ambassador for the company.

The state metaphor is obviously complicated by taking the generally private ownership of companies into account. They are often owned by people who do not participate in its organizational reality and those who represent the organization's reality are very rarely chosen by the employees themselves, or even in consultation with them. The representative of the community, that is, the leader, is also rarely formally committed to being held accountable to the employees; indeed, is often not even really responsible to them, but rather to a board, unless he himself chooses to cultivate such a relationship. Nonetheless, the state metaphor is useful because it can emphasize that rights and duties go together in the relations between employees, leaders and the organization. Also, the demand for legitimation of decisions, among other means, by a critical examination of their consequences for various employees and stakeholder groups, ought to be unconditional.

But the metaphors are mixed. The problem with values-based management as a concept is that contains many programs that combine state metaphors with metaphors of church and family. One might disagree about when it is appropriate to construe the organization as one big family. And we have recently seen a flood of critiques of the conflation of the personal convictions of individuals with the demands that the company makes to the content of its "spirit". Even when it seems immediately beneficial to the bottom line, the protestant mindset generally finds organizational brainwashing abhorrent and is inclined to see it in the operation of such metaphors.

But behind these differences a very realistic dilemma conceals itself. We all know that personal development is necessary in order to carry out the work demanded by hypermodern organizations and that this is especially necessary when it comes to leadership. For the moment the whole catalogue of universal personal attributes—what we call "human attributes"—becomes decisive in a work setting because the work demands focus areas such as empathy, passion, visionary talents and the ability to think along lines of social responsibility then the company *must* overlap with the home. After all, the dilemma consists in the fact that one can only develop one's individuality in one's working life if one is subject to the demands of the community. This is owed to the fact that the duty to the community is a prerequisite for integration into precisely the tasks that can develop one's skills and personality.

The problem then becomes one of how the organization can encourage individuals to do something *for* the company, and to do something that is really only their own business. It must also encourage them to do the opposite: to do something for themselves that is really of interest only to the company.

In the rest of this book the metaphorical burden will carried largely by the "state" and the "arts". But we can't get around the metaphor of the stage, the role, the theatre—it is unavoidable. I will, that is, simply try to avoid succumbing to the metaphors of the religion and family when dealing with the relationship between leaders, employees and organizations.

Chapter 15

The New Language of Leadership

In the preceding chapter I have gone through a metaphorical framework for thinking about modern management and organization. I here concluded that this metaphor, which is concentrated around the society of the state, was best suited to maintain the tension between the personal interests of both the leader and the employees, on the one hand, and, on the other, the demands that stem from the organization as a real and formal community.

The metaphor of a state society can maintain the legitimacy of decisions as the horizon against which the individual leader appropriate authoritative forms of the power of position. Legitimacy builds on consent that is justified in the light of complete information about ends and means. But it is also built on *recognition* as a way in which management confirms that its legitimate decisions have been understanding and have been implemented in the intended manner.

It is natural, then, to emphasize that the leadership is first and foremost distinguished from what preceded it through its relation to the entire *strategic* field.

For it is characteristic of state societies that its leaders can operate on the basis of a proxy that is given to them on two grounds:

- Their will and ability to embody the "constitution" of the organization.
- The fact they in principle report to directly to each member of the organization, as is the case in a direct democracy.

The moment the metaphor of a state society is understood within the framework of *direct democracy*, the significance of the organizational structures as "representative" filters for the communication of power and legitimacy begins to fade. The leader no longer has any buffers or blind spots in the organization that can serve as excuses for the fact that the organization does not function as one big, living organism, permeated by foundation of common values that is expresses in the company's manifesto.

Here we run into a paradox that is connected with the new leadership: the leader, by virtue of the need to delegate responsibility to others is given increased responsibility for everything that happens in the intermediating layers of the company.

But we run into yet another paradox in the exercise of leadership. As the significance of visions and values increases, that is, as the organization's means to appear suggestively and expressively in its inner spaces are strengthened, meaning that images, stories and examples become increasingly important in the daily routines of the company, the demands on the leader increases to counterbalance these aesthetic elements.

The rhetorical and poetic horizon for the communication of inner cohesion obviously constitutes a danger, as we have seen it in the totalitarian regimes of the preceding century, where it precisely all these non-discursive elements (images, insignia, uniforms, battle hymns) played an enormous role in the indoctrination of social identity. The leader must be a guarantor for the communication of information that is not subject to the aesthetization of communication, that is, the advances that push the true, the just and the good out of the beautiful so that the beautiful can serve power by its many facets.

One could here be tempted to say that the leader ought to be a kind of *philosopher*, because philosophy has, since the time of Plato, been the precisely the area where the critique of rhetorical and poetical means has been most forcefully articulated. Philosophy urges caution about expressions that speak only to the emotions. The philosopher has been exceptionally aware of his use of concepts and of media to articulate his message and his thoughts.

The leader must, in other words, resist the temptation to re-enchant organizational reality.

The Stoics were especially conscious of this. Zeno, one of the founders of stoic philosophy, established the following ideals for the use of language by philosophers.

- To speak proper Greek (English) devoid of vulgarity and exaggeration.
- To express oneself clearly so that the idea is presented with the aim of being understood as well as is possible.
- To be precise, applying a minimalism in the form of expression, so that no superfluous concepts are used.

- To be relevant, so that the style suits that which is sought to be expressed.
- Acuity, so that clichés, slogans and easy imagery are avoided.[14]

In other words, if the metaphor of state society is to be applied to the organization, then the leader must not speak as a pork-barreling politician.

That means, then, that the leader must be conscious of the metaphorical framework that he refers to in his speaking. He may appeal to metaphors but he must make it clear that that is what he is doing. Images and metaphors are in that sense not performative or strategic effects but rough sketches of a new understanding, which can be received by the listener by consenting to a particular interpretation of the situation. The metaphor thereby ceases to be an instrument of power but is rather, in a profound sense, part of a movement toward the contours of accord. But accord must not be confused with consensus because consensus often presupposes both bitter abstraction from actual emotional distances and a series of argumentative compromises. Perfect consensus obviously does not exist in organizations with more than three members, and when it does happen it is often in relation to basic facts or platitudes. Accord, by contrast, is a condition that does not pretend that it does not involve price.

To be in accord with someone or with a situation is to be prepared to relinquish the objects of one's personal ambition, but it does *not* mean that one has to force oneself to live with a compromise. If one is in accord, then one is in agreement.

The aforementioned rules for conscious, non-rhetorical use of language creates a constant language through maximum reflection by the one that is speaking. But this reflection must be shared with the listener. This sort of "new puritanism" is a very large demand to make of a leader but it can be accomplished—Winston Churchill had this ability—and it *must* be accomplished if the inner atmosphere of the company is not to become hollow or, worse, cloying and claustrophobic.

We can obviously also just say that the leader must necessarily educate himself and become a truly great orator. For great oratory overcomes the petty props and effects of rhetoric.

---

[14] Cf. Diogenes Laertius. *Lives of Eminent Philosophers*. Book VVII, 59-60. Loeb, Harvard University Press, 1995, Vol II.

The first competence that the leader must develop is a sense of the situation and its context. He must *a sense of the situation in order to create the event.*

The strongest reference point for what is said lies it the shared world which the leader must be able to evoke with a moment's notice in its clear and tangible outline. The summation includes the prompt to action, in so far as it can occur in the light of common set of metaphors, which are always available in the vision and values that make up the discoverable core of common values. We can also say that the leader is at a given moment capable of maintaining a sense of *the common project* in even the most minute decisions.

Chapter 16

The Leader as a Spiritual Lighthouse

Let me now try to shed some light on these ideas about normative leadership by relating them to a series of problems that arise in connection with public and private management in *the knowledge society*.

The high rate of progress in the knowledge society makes new demands on the public identity of the leader in four ways:

- Public administration as a workplace
- The relationship between public administration and the individual citizen
- The relationship between public administration and the private sphere (stakeholders in the market).
- The public administration's relation to global society

This brings tendencies to the fore that have been at work in private business for a long time, namely, an increased focus on HRM strategies, the redirecting sales activities toward individuals, not segments of the population, the development of values based arguments for the existence of an organization, the construal of the company in global terms, whether according to market, culture or manufacture of a viable public image.

In the public sphere, this picture is complicated by the fact that these areas are increasingly intertwined with each other but without giving the leader even an approximation of the means that are available in private business, and without the needed will to change the organizational structures that are in place. It is clear that projects involving private and public "entrepreneurs" cooperating on an equal footing will be able to provide a new form not just for the construction of public works but also for the maintenance and daily operations. The reasonable counter to privatization seems to be sharing within the framework of task specific "conglomerations". The new public leader must have the traits of both the entrepreneur and the negotiator. But to get it started to undertake the necessary experiments is more difficult and more daring.

The administration, taken as a workplace, is characterized by contradictions. On the one hand we have a culture of negotiation and consensus based on the leader's ability to foster *legitimacy* in regard to particular decisions. The leader must be able to balance the preferences of internal interest groups against broader political concerns. The leader must, that is, be able to combine insight into political aspects of decisions with a comprehensive technical survey of a situation. For example, the demands of the government minister to increase rate at which cases are processed may be in conflict with standard administrative practice or with personnel policies. Here the leader must choose a criterion and take the heat.

On the other hand, there is a decision context that must relinquish its bonds to a legitimacy founded on consensus because the parameters for the decision are too contradictory and uncertain. Here the leader must cut through the complexities of the situation according to *his own* image of the future task tasks of the administration regardless of the reigning politicians or boards. Personal, normative authority is a necessity. In Denmark, we had an example of this when the Director General of the Environmental Protection Agency stepped down as a result of serious budget cutbacks for the agency. He did not want to take responsibility (which *would become* his) of for implementing these budget reductions. In the business world, the case of the new CEO of Lundbeck, Claus Bræstrup, is of interest. He carried out a depreciation of the stock of the company at great cost to the shareholders at the time—no doubt including himself. The leader had to have the courage to begin anew.

A decisive side of the new leadership will consists in the leaders ability to foster solutions that either entirely or partially dissolve existing organizational structures or creates new structures by transgressing habitual administrative boundaries. It is possible, for example, to gather education, business and culture in a single administrative unit or develop the idea of a "project hotel" to support regional innovation across sectors, or an "experimentarium". The leader must here be able to present the visionary energy of new concept to both politicians and users. It is also possible to build an innovation strategy on the direct articulation of the customer's needs, so the customer becomes consultant.

The Leader as a Spiritual Lighthouse

What makes the knowledge society different from previous societies is the decisive condition that knowledge is no longer strongly tied to ideologies, and that every decision is always forced into a space of possibilities where it is measured on the scales of the future, which it is itself a shaper of. The age of long-term planning is over. Moreover, it is no longer possible to offer casual references to "ideological rationality". The public sector can longer engage in planning because the world has grown too virtual. The leader must therefore be able to foster both visions and convincing images of their sustainability. Paradoxically, the image and the story, that is, visual elements, replace argument in the knowledge society. We know so much that concepts and logical deductions become insufficient, indeed, suspect as the basis of decision making.

The leader must in the sense be able to lead the experimentations in which knowledge is transformed into concrete visions. The form of address that must be adopted by the new leader is no longer "Listen!" but "Look!" and perhaps even "Feel!" and this in the sense of both of "Take a hold of the future with your hands!" ("Build a model out of Lego blocks!", "Use the keyboard to construct a graphic representation of the scenario and *look at it* on the walls inside the dome which is the firmament of the future!"), *and* "Get in touch with your inner selves!" Or even simple "Try it! Apply it in your own lives!"

The public and private leader ought to be able together to enter into a productive spiral and here compete for the exploitation of new possibilities.

But another and more important theme now emerges on the scene. In private business we already have a sense of this: the leader must become a philosopher. Not just because philosophy traditionally also takes a critical stance with respect to images and stories, and to the enchanting power in the tools of rhetoric and poetry, but also because the philosopher traditionally has the courage to be guided by his own "wisdom". It takes a profound grounding in the personal communicative potentials to be able to establish a clear and suggestive discourse as an alternative to images and stories. This is something the leader in the public sector must also learn.

In a world that does not just change to the beat of a jitterbug, but where the firm characteristics of previous times—technology and bureaucracy—and thereby the historicity of block-solid decisions erodes, the public leader, as the private, must believe in himself. But this self-confidence can't be born by a by a strain act of self-creation—it must be firmly grounded.

The Virtue of Leadership

In the past, it was procedure that grounded us in administration. Today, however, processes are replacing procedures—which were never anything other than the anticipation and summary of processes and thereby often an unfortunate closing of realms of possibility.

Process-oriented leadership presupposes and brings with it a space of freedom for the involved parties. The greater this space is the greater the potential for creativity, but the greater is also the risk. The opening of a space of freedom for employees always presupposes trust in the professional skills and commitment of the employees, but skill is itself up for grabs in the knowledge society because there are so many different, but theoretically and experimentally justified, ways in which given tasks can be completed. There are, no doubt, as many pedagogical theories and experiments to justify early socialization of children in kinder gardens as there are theories that say the opposite. Likewise, there are presumably as many arguments for a relatively long and uncontrolled development phase in the innovation process as there are arguments for the value of early goal-oriented guidance.

The fact that the knowledge society confronts us with so many good reasons for very different ways to proceed and the fact that these reasons are seriously grounded scientific attitudes or "paradigms" puts the leader in a very difficult position. Politicians need to help themselves through "rational" models of reality that everyone (including themselves) knows are truncated ("free initiative," for example—has this ever existed in practice?). Or they must appeal to values that are conspicuously irrational.

The leader must in a sense remain aloof in the face of these reasons and all these different ideologies and values, unless he wants to resign himself to being and ideology or an administrator of the bottom line alone. This may seem admirable in its honesty, but everyone knows that he is wasting an opportunity—or perhaps even betraying the future.

The problem here is that the personal history that gives even the manager with a one-track mind an aura of professional authority is not always available to the leader in the public sector to the same degree, even if one has the technical administration bug. Nor can the professional top manager always have the professional commitment it takes to lead his company to the front of the pack. After all, he could be the head many different kinds of company, indicating that something must be necessarily be missing.

It is precisely the fact of being a professionally qualified generalist or a generally grounded expert that is facing hard time in today's

The Leader as a Spiritual Lighthouse

society. There are good reasons for this because there exists no "studium generale" in the knowledge society. The leader can be educated at the best institutions of higher learning, he can have a PhD in economics from Harvard, but at the end of the day it is only his good will and his experience that he can depend on.

In this sense it is important that the leader can learn from his own practice. It becomes wholly decisive that the leader has a set of ideas about what it means to lead. But these ideas all too easily become "tools", and tools are the opposite of a communicative and visionary sensibility. The leader is simply in need of inner benchmarks that are at the same time quite universal in order to be able learn from what he is doing. These benchmarks have been the characteristics of the West for 3000 years. They are found in the Greek Square: goodness, justice, beauty and truth. The public leader who does not take these as his guide will never amount to more that "Mr. So-and-So, the administrator" or "manager" in terms of his own career. And a leader in private business who can't read the writing on the wall can do enormous damage to a company because the market and therefore the public has begun to differentiate between companies that exploit society, in order to make a fast buck, and companies that understand their social responsibilities.

In this sense, the *attitude* toward personal leadership that makes serious management possible in the knowledge society cannot get around being *normative*. The leader must have an ideal of the coming society and about the reality "behind" the social and as such in order to be able to grow through his leadership, which is able to assign "the human factor" a place of privilege.

There are five big questions. *What* are we going to do? *Why* should we do it? (Can we leave it undone or do something better?) *How* are we going to do it? *Who* should do it? *How* will we measure whether we have done it well enough? These questions, which all good leadership manages to comprehend in a single gesture, can not be dealt with in a satisfactory manner by way of tools. The tied to situations and context and can therefore to happy and unhappy circumstances. They are bound to timing, to the ability to give incidents and accidents a chance to have an effect, to empathy, and to communicative sensitivity. They are bound to the leader's opportunity to let his actions carry their normative weight. These questions can therefore only be given answers if their expression is bound to a visionary style of leadership which can serve as an exemplary form of validity in public administration and in the business community, which is satisfying in the knowledge society. It is all about providing *examples* of successful leadership.

Here a historical note is in order. The word "official" comes from the Latin "officium", which means both "duty" and "post". We know the unification of these meaning in the traditional role of the "civil servant", but the word "officium" is a Latin translation of the Greek concept of "katékon", which was undertaken by the Roman philosopher Cicero. Like a true roman citizen he shifted the meaning of the concept into the sphere of the state, but the Greek concept, which stems from Stoic philosophy, has a broader and deeper meaning. It referred to all those actions that a human being ought to carry out in the interest of others and with an eye to his own universal humanity. Among these are a concern for the family, for the aged, for nature, and for society. It is the combined responsible for a society held in common. It is the responsibility to make life meaningful, to do one's job and to keep one's finances in order.

The new leader, in the public sector and in private business, cannot and should not become a new kind of civil servant, but he can become a kind of a "official" within this broad spectrum of human value, which when view historically is built into the concept of "kathékon"—the set of virtues that lead to the good life.

The leader must subscribe to the great tradition of European humanism by conceiving of the market as a part of the public sphere in which we are shaped in order to desire and realize the good life as such.

When the public sector therefore begins to address its citizens as "users", the private ought to compensate by addressing its customers as "citizens". The knowledge society transforms the market into a new public space as long as information from both public and private spheres is commoditized through new forms of interaction. When the user is able to seek new information about his rights in the public institutions and be given cause to take his case in his own hands directly, *and* when he of his own impulse investigates the history of the products he buys, including the detailed scrutiny of the "criminal records" the companies who supply them, then the concept of market is embroiled in the concept of information, which naturally implies normative criteria are including in the assessment of products along with technical and economic criteria.

From the point of view of the knowledge society, this is a profoundly rational attitude, because the users of the public sector will of course increasingly conceive of themselves as holders of rights by way of their humanity as knowledge is spread through education and communication. But this notion of rights will also be transferred to the products and services of private business. The user has a right to products that are part of the image of the good life, not just in their consumption but also in their production.

When global positions cease to be able to enter into political discourse unless they do so through the language of "humanity", it also begins to count for companies that want to establish themselves on the world market. If not, they will come to be run by insensitive and self-centered national and multinational interests.

Finally, the dialogue between the public and the private, which is intensifying, and being sharpened and deepened through closer contact and thereby through greater understanding of each other's worlds can only proceed within the framework of an articulated concern for our shared society and reality, through this language of "humanity".

The new leader must, in other words, become a true humanist. A human being that through his own example encourages the formative processes of learning and to the shaping of the self through the development of an acute sensibility for social justice at all levels in all events.

Chapter 17

The Twelve Virtues of Leadership

The clearest and most tangible way to account for the nerve of the new leadership is to tie the relationship between the leader and the norms to the concept of *virtue*.

A virtue is an attitude that commits because human beings have invested their whole existence in it.

A virtue implies that the relation to "values" establishes commitments. Thus virtues prevent the reification of values, i.e., the process of turning them into things, which can be measured, adjusted for strategic purposes, or negotiated and, occasionally, prostituted. The political moralist, who uses values as a costume or as the elements of a dossier or as excuses, breaks the back of virtue—it remains closed to him.

In virtue, the norm and the man enter a communion that can only be broken if the individual betrays himself.

The Greek concept of *ethos*, from which "ethics" is derived, expresses this communion. As mentioned earlier, "ethos" has two basic senses. With a long "e" ("êta"), it means "character" or "personality" but also one's normative background, i.e., one's family, education and culture. With a short "e" ("epsilon") it means "the good habit" and denotes the ability to shape one's life and self in the image of the Greek Square guided by the inheritance one has in the form of talents, knowledge, integrity and norms.

The interaction of the two senses of "ethos" is the decisive force in the development of a human being's virtue. There is a built in contradiction in this, however, which Aristotle was already aware of in his ethics, and which I have already mentioned. To do good presupposes knowledge of the good, but knowledge of the good presupposed the experience of having done it.

Aristotle had a concept to denote the dissolution of this contradiction. He called it *hexis*, which is translated as "habitus" in Latin but cannot be identified with "habit" in English. On the contrary, a hexis is the whole of the normatively guided process by which a human being struggles to learn the good by practicing it in every situation. It takes courage, determination and moral imagination to do so. If one persists one slowly becomes better and better—insight, skill and sensibility settle in the spine, just as one learns to play a musical instrument. But the relapse is waiting to pounce at every turn because the instrument one is playing is one's own soul-body-reality and it is here that insight, desire and passion wait to usurp reason and social commitment.

When *hexis* is mastered the individual attains what Aristotle called *phronesis*—a wisdom that has the potential to be concrete.

There are, of course, a number of functional demands to be made of the leader, but it would be foolhardy to think that one can isolate "technical" traits of a leader such as "resolution", "decisiveness" and "consistency", which are not normative in their essence. The image of humanity presented by many "headhunters" is not just laughable but outdated. What they can produce is a throwback—the bronco buster who thinks his methods still work in a circus of stand-up comedians, magicians and mind readers.

The road to virtue passes through the three maxims of Immanuel Kant, which he articulated in his last great book, *The Critique of Judgment* (*Kritk der Urteilskraft*) from 1790.

- the ability to think critically and autonomously
- the ability to feel empathy for any other human being
- being in accord with oneself

The last maxim is the dominant one and it is this one that shows us what we can expect of the will in our attempts to live the virtuous life. But it is a long road to the stage where the soul's conversation with itself is conducted with a steady, completely harmonious voice. It is the road to an inner unity and there are no guarantees in the world of virtue. It comes at a cost.

The twelve virtues are relatively complex. Each of them depends on the demands of the event, but they must all be mastered if a human being is to attain great leadership.

I have decided not to provide contemporary examples of leaders that embody the virtues. The only face we should be seeing before us when we consider the virtues of leadership is our own.

The virtues are built around the Greek virtues because this makes their connection to the Greek Square as clear as possible and because philosophy allows us to establish the greatest possible distance from the standing threat of reigning buzzwords. This approach grants us a measure of precision. But the virtues are intended as at least potentially and will hopefully be understood as such.

The First Virtue of Leadership
To be the servant of the community
At his inauguration, the pope bows before the assembled masses and declares that he is "servus servorum", the servant of the servant.

We have already encountered the concepts that characterize the first virtue of leadership since they stem from Plato's characterization of in the *Statesman*. Transferred to the organization, it looks as follows:

Trophé: the sense of responsibility for the organization as a whole and for the individual.

The Greek concept refers to the "shepherd", but this seems to us to be too pompous, too patriarchal, and too pastoral.

Below "trophé", Plato placed two additional virtues.

Therapeia: the ability to grant and receive recognition.

The concept of therapy has some unfortunate connotations in the context of leadership, but its original meaning is to help human beings to help themselves. It can make sense in an organizational context, even if "therapeuo" is translated as "seductio" in Latin, i.e., seduction, as long as we insist on the idea that the form of seduction practiced by a leader is one that secures the conditions under which the individual can be led back to himself.

Therapeia is therefore about help into self-help and about realistic feedback. It is central to the delegation of responsibility because it presupposes a level-headed assessment of the employees' strengths and weaknesses.

The other subordinate concept is *epimeleia*. In Latin, it becomes "cura", which we know in English as "care". The care for the life of the individual, both inside and outside the organization, can even today seem a bit claustrophobic, so it is important to execute this function with restraint and moderation.

The Second Virtue of Leadership
Autonomy
This leadership virtue presupposes the independence and personal integrity that originates from the clarity of a person's motives in his choice of the role of leader.

A certain "autarchy" is connected to this—an ability to stand by the choices one makes and thereby to go the distance. The choice as a leader is based on personal principles and, not least, on a genuine regard for the community. The leader cannot be an egoist, even though he has a right to be concerned about his resume. His attitude is characterized by inner harmony.

A clear normative species of awareness follows from autonomy, an elucidation of the norms to which one is responsible and which one ought to realize through one's work.

Autonomy brings ethical integrity. The leader is a moral politician, not a political moralist.

Autonomy has no fear of dialogue but is always ready and able to account unconditionally for the legitimacy of its decisions.

The Third Virtue of Leadership
Equity
This virtue has its Greek paradigm in Aristotle's concept of *epieikeia*, which expresses the generosity that those who have power can show for those they have in their power. This concept is translated as "aequitas" in Latin, which figured in Roman law to emphasize the duty of the judge to take the situation of the accused at the time of the crime into consideration.

Equity demands that the leader is faithful to the spirit of the law, not primarily its letter. He has the courage to interpret the organization's written and unwritten laws with regard to the employee.

The equitable leader cannot just offer sober and level-headed criticism: he is also able to receive it.

Honesty and trust are attitudes that are justly attributed to him, and which he can expect in return.

The Fourth Virtue of Leadership
Practical wisdom, phronesis
This virtue, which obviously presupposes experience with leadership, expresses the leader's ability to find a balance between psychological insight, realistic sense of the situation and principled action.

Wisdom is in no way connected with something contemplative or abstract. The wise man is realistic without being cynical. He is level-headed without being cold. And he is a carrier of the utopian power that is possessed only by people who have experienced so much that he believes in well prepared miracles.

Wisdom is obviously the generalist's mark of honor. It is his true qualification.

The Fifth Virtue of Leadership
Judgment, eubulia
This virtue is emphasized by Plato in the *Statesman* as the most important ability of philosophical leaders. It really means "well advised"—but he was hardly thinking of spin doctors.

Judgment involves a comprehensive sense of the community, which anticipates both inner and outer conflicts before they arise. It has a pronounced sense of the ways in which a balance between inner and outer pressures in the organization is established.

Judgment presupposes a notable sense of history, and an ability to apply both the mistakes and successes that others have experienced.

"Eubulia" is also a sense of what is possible. It is the ability to find escape routes and alternatives.

It is a talent of generalists, just like *phronesis*, because it is able to see the craftsmanship that its discourses are embroiled in from a higher level.

Judgment is voiced beyond the "rhetorical machines". It speaks in a sparse language and loves minimalist dialogues.

The Sixth Virtue of Leadership
The Art of Midwifery, majeutics
Socrates claimed that he was the son of a midwife and a sculptor. The first delivers both the child and the mother. The other removes the superfluous material from the slab of stone.

Majeutics is an expression of intelligent empathy. But it is also dangerous because it can manipulate. It demands seriousness to control it if one is really good at it.

The ability to put yourself in another's place does not have to paralyze you. On the contrary, attention, dialogical intensity and consistency, human warmth and humor all give room for self-management. But the leader must also respect the space between us—the space that is always found between two speakers, which those who are unable to modulate their power and their will to power so easily intimidate.

The Seventh Virtue of Leadership
A sense of time and the ability to seize the moment, kairos-pathos
It is said that "Kairos" was in Greece depicted as a young men with a tuft of hair in on his forehead. As he ran towards one, one could grab it

if one was quick enough, otherwise the opportunity was lost. There was no tuft of hair on his neck.

It is a sense of the situation and an awareness of context; the whole capacity to be ready for the event belongs under this virtue.

It demands courage, steadfastness and patience.

Chora is also attached to kairos. It is the Greek word for space or spatiality, a "boundless territory" to contrast with "topos"—the local.

The *chorological* capacity expresses the sense of place in time and time in place. As a virtue it consists in the will to be loyal to the place and in the ability to come into contact with all that has been handed down to and inhabits a place, for better or for worse. The relationship between companies, administrations and institutions as abstract "machines" and the buildings, neighborhoods and areas that house them, along with the history of these entities themselves, are all things that the leader must a sense of. We often call institutions by the places where they are. The leader must also have as sense of the organization's physical space, and thereby its atmosphere. He must have a sense of how far physical changes can be taken, and who is affected by them.

The Eighth Virtue of Leadership
Immediate insight, epibolé
In Latin, it is called "intuition". No one knows what it is, but the Greeks associated it with rhetorical forms of inference in which one is so daring or so fearless as to omit some of the premises. Later, this form inference has been proposed as the logic of invention and innovation, and has been called "abduction" by the American philosopher C. S. Peirce.

But even if one can choose to take a broad view of the missing premises, one cannot select the situations from which these premises are missing. It just happens. What you can do, is to ennoble your experiences. Intuition, in any case, happens at a level of consciousness in which is hidden most of what we have either forgotten or don't even know we have seen and heard. But the ennobling of experience is associated with the art of interpretation, because the more we understand of what happens to us, of that which others achieve or accomplish, all the more impoverished can all that which we have hitherto experienced come to be because it appears in another light.

But the best way to develop intuition is to use it.

The Ninth Virtue of Leadership
Euphoria
This is the virtue of the epicurean philosophers: "to take adversity lightly", to cultivate "eudymia", the joy of the inevitable.

We could call this virtue simply a "sense of reality", because it makes possible the act of daring that faith is, the fact that reality can be different in a positive sense.

If a leader possesses this virtue it is doubtless contagious because it releases enthusiasm without loss of freedom.

It is the poetic sense, the capacity to create the reality that we are all drawn into.

As attitude, euphoria is close to hope.

The Tenth Virtue of Leadership
Articulateness, hermeneia
Hermes, who has granted his name to the word, was the God that communicated messages between the living and the dead. But he was also the God of merchants and thieves. He is responsible for fair trade in meaning; he keeps what is said in circulation and steals the occasional smile.

This virtue is important for a leader, because it is he that in the final analysis has responsibility for the communication of the organization's message; that is, he must see to it that it is understood.

He must be willing and able to explain; he must strive to foster understanding. Here the leader becomes almost a teacher.

But it is also about the will to eradicate the manipulation of meaning and eschew indoctrination. It is about resisting totalitarianism.

Hermeneia is the virtue that resists the temptations of branding and avoids its traps.

It is, not least, through the demands it makes of the leader that he feels culture as a challenge; and it is through culture that he begins to be a humanist.

The Eleventh Virtue of Leadership
To understand organizing
Forces are constantly at work in every organization. There is a flow that consists in many different processes, with different inherent times. It is the leader's task to serve this flow, this "nisus", this power, and it presupposes that he has a sense of it.

He has to help this new organic or revolutionary form that is prepared to come into being in this flow, and this presupposes that he can detect it, and judge it.

The leader must conquer his prejudices. He must conquer even his own expectations of his position, and then become a facilitator of this process.

In this sense, the leader is the guardian of a new order.

But he must understand that new structures that prescribe and intensify work processes always at the same time have a moment of protection in them. They should not just strengthen the leader's control, but also give the employees a space of freedom.

The Twelfth Virtue of Leadership
The leader must make the spirit of the organization tangible; he exemplifies its ethos.
He must do as he says, and be what he does.

He must forge ahead in the process where the members of the organization unite their rights and their duties.

First and foremost, he must express the very essence of leadership through his own person. There is a twist: in Old Norse, "leitha", from which the word "to lead" comes, means two things.

- To walk ahead.
- To look for something.

The leader must be the one who walks on up ahead through the doors of the Greek Square. He must also seek, and what he seeks is the unconditional.